IMAGES
of America

CAPE MAY

IN VINTAGE POST

D1280549

Light-house,
Cape May Point,
Cape May, N.J.

CAPE MAY LIGHTHOUSE, *c.* 1911. Construction began in 1857 to replace two earlier Cape May Point lighthouses lost to the elements. Until electrification in 1938, the U.S. Lighthouse Service keepers carried fuel up the 157-foot tower and maintained lens apparatus daily. An 1860 keepers' house is on the right; the 1893 oil house is on the left.

IMAGES
of America

CAPE MAY
IN VINTAGE POSTCARDS

Don and Pat Pocher

ARCADIA

First printed in 1998.
Reprinted in 2000, 2001, 2002.

Published by Arcadia Publishing,
an imprint of Tempus Publishing, Inc.
2A Cumberland Street
Charleston, SC 29401

Printed in Great Britain.

For all general information contact Arcadia Publishing at:
Telephone 843-853-2070
Fax 843-853-0044
E-Mail sales@arcadiapublishing.com

For customer service and orders:
Toll-Free 1-888-313-2665

Visit us on the internet at http://www.arcadiapublishing.com

THORNTON POCHER, 1904. This raggedy real photo postcard of the author's father was discovered during the 1980s, tucked away with others in a shoebox at the family home on South Lafayette Street. That small treasure trove of cards sent by little Popo from Cape May to his father in New York became the catalyst for the collection illustrating this book.

Contents

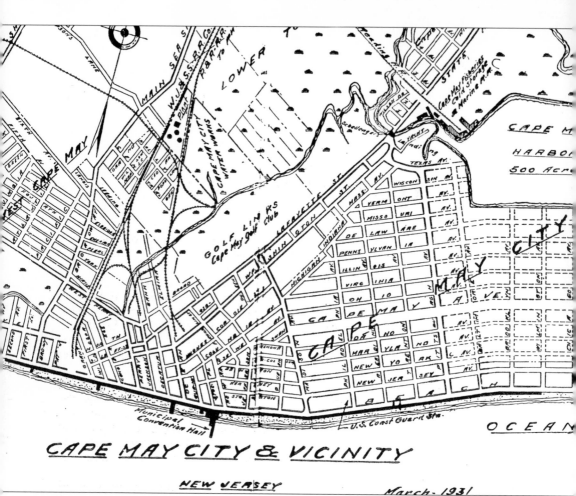

CAPE MAY CITY & VICINITY

NEW JERSEY

March - 1931

MAP FOR ORIENTATION. Notice that many of the streets in early Cape May were named for presidents and military leaders: Washington, Madison, Jackson, Grant, Lafayette, and Decatur, for example. Planners of the east end's New Cape May chose to name streets for cities and states to stress that this development was of national interest.

Introduction

When the 20th century was young, visitors to Cape May, New Jersey knew exactly how to show the folks back home the attractions, accommodations, and ambiance of the nation's oldest seaside resort—they sent a penny postcard.

Publishers provided a vast choice of views, capturing white sands crowded with colorful tents and wool-suited bathers or the beachfront Stockton, Lafayette, and Congress Hall Hotels with their towering white columns. Popular postcards depicted the Casino, Red Mill, the Corinthian Yacht Club, the Fun Factory, the Convention Hall, and the Cape May Point Lighthouse. Reprinted Victorian views of hotels destroyed by fire served as reminders of the resort's glory days. Real photo cards chronicled newsworthy events including the creation of the harbor, the construction of huge modern Hotel Cape May, and the 1907 fire at the Iron Pier.

Postcards were mass produced for the first time in America in 1893 for the World's Columbian Exposition in Chicago. Before you could sing "Meet Me in St. Louis, Looey," the proliferation of postcards available at the next World's Fair in 1904 triggered a postcard craze. Tourists no longer had to be content with a pretty view printed on a paper card. They could send one trimmed with silk or made of wood. Some revealed hidden pictures or glowing windows when held to the light and others had mechanical parts. How could the recipients resist saving such souvenirs?

As the selection of cards expanded to include greetings to suit almost any occasion and small town views, the number of collectors burgeoned. Friends exchanged cards, held postcard "showers," and organized clubs. Between 1906 and 1907, the Jolly Jokers expanded to 25 states and over 2,300 members, becoming America's largest postcard club.

Postcards to arrange in albums, communicate messages, or send as souvenirs could be found everywhere from corner stores to cigar stands, as well as in postcard shops. Local businessmen became publishers of hometown postcards by sending black-and-white photographs plus instructions for color schemes to city printers who, prior to World War I, often shipped them to Germany to be printed on sophisticated presses.

Here in Cape May, postcards from over 25 different publishers were sold, but the leader was entrepreneur Joseph K. Hand, a paperhanger whose father and grandfather were prominent jewelers specializing in Cape May diamonds. On a 1909 card, he describes himself as "Importer and Jobber of Postcards." His publisher of choice was the Albertype Company of Brooklyn, New York. Both collectors and residents treasure these hand-colored images of old Cape May.

Between 1903 and 1913, the Golden Age of postcards, thousands of penny postcards were mailed from Cape May. Thanks to packrats and collectors, an amazing percentage of these have survived. In *Cape May*, we offer a small sample of these vintage postcards, retrieved and researched, so that you can rediscover pre-World War II Cape May and explore the rich heritage that entitles this resort to be designated a National Landmark City.

Don and Pat Pocher, 1998

Acknowledgments

In 1992, we utilized postcards from our collection as the nucleus of the Greater Cape May Historical Society's first summer exhibit at the Colonial House, "World War I & Cape May." The exhibits have become an annual event and the number of collaborators contributing memories and memorabilia has grown lengthy. I'm grateful to the Greater Cape May Historical Society for giving me the privilege of acting as curator, a challenging educational experience that helped give us the background and confidence to write this book.

One of the joys of our hobby is the fellowship that exists among postcard collectors. Illustrations are marked with the initials of both old and new friends who were kind enough to share choice postcards from their collections. They are as follows: the Cape May County Historical Society (CMCHS), Walter Homan Campbell (WHC), Ed DeHaven (EDH), Robert W. Elwell Sr. (RE), "Capt. Flukebuggy" (FB), Richard Gibbs (RG), and Mike and Sandy Wieber (M&SW).

As we wrote the captions, we turned to a network of generous local historians, including Sara "Sue" Hughes Leaming—the matriarch of Cape May historians; John Nash—steward of Cape May's Afro-American heritage; H. Gerald MacDonald—railroad and Coast Guard consultant; and Larry R. Paul—Hotel Cape May researcher.

Several out-of-print books were our most valuable sources of information. They included The Albert Hand Company's 1937 *A Book of Cape May*; Robert C. Alexander's articles and his 1956 *Ho! For Cape Island!*; George Thomas and Carl Doebley's 1976 edition of *Cape May—Queen of the Seaside Resorts*—essential for architectural data; and the 1942 *History of Cape May N.J. Section Base, U.S. Navy, 25th Anniversary*.

Finally, Don and I wish to thank Kelly—patient proofreader of the manuscript, and Mom—provider of moral support and inspirational home-cooking.

Pat Pennington Pocher, 1998

One

Historic
Accommodations

What was reputed at that time to be the largest Hotel in the world, the Mount Vernon was destroyed by fire on the night of September 5th 1856, the proprietor and four other persons losing their lives in the flames. The Dining-Room accommodated 3,000 people.

HISTORICAL CAPE MAY.

MOUNT VERNON HOTEL.

MOUNT VERNON HOTEL, *c.* 1853. About 1911, Joseph K. Hand used old engravings and photographs for a series of at least six cards illustrating early hotels lost to fire. Started in 1852 on 10 beachfront acres near Broadway, the monumental Mount Vernon boasted hot and cold running water, a gasworks, pistol galleries, ten-pin alleys, and accommodations for 2,100 before its blazing post-season devastation.

UNITED STATES HOTEL, BUILT 1853. Today a book store stands where A.W. Tompkins built this grand hotel at Washington and Decatur Streets. One windy August morning in 1869, a fire that began at the nearby Pearl Diver's curio shop quickly engulfed the hotel and its neighbors. Fortunately, Camden sent volunteer firemen and apparatus 90 miles by train to "extinguish the raging flames."

NEW ATLANTIC, c. 1848. This victim of the 1869 fire was built on the east side of Jackson Street by Philadelphia's McMakin brothers, Delaware Bay steamboat owners. The Atlantic was the first Cape Island hotel with a painted exterior. Long rows of tables accommodated 350 diners in its 100-foot-long hall and the upper floors held 300 lodgers.

OCEAN HOUSE. Cape May's Great Fire began in this vacant Perry Street hotel at about 7 a.m. on November 9, 1878, shortly after proprietor Samuel Ludlam had left his insured establishment for Philadelphia. Firemen struggled to subdue the flames that swept rapidly from building to building, destroying over 35 acres by evening.

CENTRE HOUSE, COMPLETED 1840. It was still morning when the fire jumped back across Perry Street from its second victim, Congress Hall, to envelop Jeremiah Mecray's hotel, shown here with its Jackson Street wing on the left and tall columns extending along Washington Street to Perry on the right. The loss was estimated at $35,000.

11

Old Congress Hall destroyed by fire 1878.   CAPE MAY, N. J.

CONGRESS HALL, *c.* 1875. When Thomas H. Hughes built the first large hotel on Cape Island in 1816, dubious residents nicknamed it Tommy's Folly. Hughes's election to Congress inspired the present name. Shown here is the enlarged frame 1854 building, which sat on 7 acres stretching from South Lafayette Street to the beach, and from Perry to Congress Street. (M&SW.)

Photo. by GILBERT & BACON, 40 N. 8th St. Philad'a.

STEREOSCOPE SLIDE: "VIEWS OF CAPE MAY AFTER THE FIRE, NOV. 9, 1878." "Rear Congress Hall" is penciled on the back of this double-image card, which looks from Perry past Congress Street's Neafie villa to the Grant Street Summer Station. Wind direction spared the west end from destruction. We prize the behind-the-chimney glimpse of our South Lafayette Street home.

Congress Hall   Cape May, N. J.

CONGRESS HALL, *c*. 1918. A stock company had purchased Congress Hall at J.F. Cake's sheriff's sale for $60,000 just six months before the fire. In 1879, E.C. Knight and associates rushed to rebuild both the hotel and the pier in time for the tourist season. This hall was of brick, smaller, and closer to the beach.

LOBBY, CONGRESS HALL.   CAPE MAY, N. J.

CONGRESS HALL LOBBY, *c*. WORLD WAR I. Some out-of-town newspapers were optimistic in the wake of the Great Fire: "With new hotels, new men and fresh blood, Cape May's future may be brighter than ever." Indeed, this massive rebuilding would one day qualify Cape May as a National Landmark. Most of the elegant Congress Hall lobby has recently been converted to shops. (RE.)

13

COLUMBIA HOUSE, BUILT 1846. Captain George Hildreth chose swampy meadow between Ocean and Decatur Streets for his hotel. By 1850, it had expanded to be the largest and most "aristocratic" on Cape Island. Though Columbia House escaped the 1869 fire, it could not be saved in 1878. Owner John Bullitt's $55,000 insurance covered most of the loss.

CHALFONTE HOTEL, c. 1907. Col. Henry Sawyer, builder of the Chalfonte in 1876, turned in the alarm for the Great Fire. The conflagration never reached his Howard Street hotel and the Chalfonte has continued to welcome guests to its gingerbread-trimmed verandahs ever since. Sawyer's fame as a Confederate prisoner saved from a "lottery of death" endures, along with his hotel's reputation for Southern hospitality. (M&SW.)

STEREOSCOPE SLIDE: "VIEWS OF CAPE MAY AFTER THE FIRE, NOV. 9, 1878." Although two Stockton Row cottages caught fire and embers landed on the Stockton Hotel roof, firemen managed to halt the flames here at Guerney Street. The ruins are the bathhouses whose pumps, disconnected for the winter, were as useless as the hotels' artesian wells and the firemen's faulty hose.

Stockton Hotel, Cape May, N. J.

STOCKTON HOTEL, *c.* 1908. This mammoth survivor of the Great Fire occupied the entire block from Guerney to Howard Streets, from Columbia Avenue to the beach where the property had been under water until filled. When the West Jersey Railroad opened the Stockton in 1869, at a cost of $600,000 to stockholders, it was considered America's largest hotel. By 1910, it was deemed obsolete and was razed.

GIRLS FRIENDLY HOLIDAY HOUSE. CAPE MAY, N. J

BALTIMORE HOTEL, BUILT *c.* 1868. One of about 17 smaller hotels remaining after the Great Fire, this three-story frame building at 642 Hughes Street was described in 1882 as one of the resort's oldest summer houses, with "all the real and solid comforts of a private home." The tall columns and simple shape illustrated on this *c.* 1940 card typify early Cape Island hotel style (see p. 84).

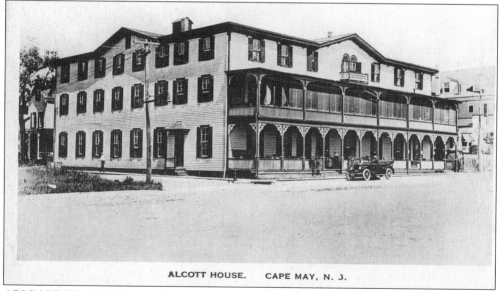

ALCOTT HOUSE.   CAPE MAY, N. J.

ARLINGTON HOTEL, BUILT 1878. John Kromer of Baltimore had this 60-room hotel constructed right across from the Grant Street railroad station platforms. Known as the Wellington in 1911, on this 1920 postcard the hotel's namesake was a popular author. Alcott House catered to working-class women and their children. Weekly rates in 1935 ranged from $9 to $15 for room and board.

WINDSOR HOTEL, *c*. 1909. As part of the rebirth of the city after the fire, architect Stephen D. Button was hired to expand Thomas Whitney's Congress Street cottage in 1879. The hotel later grew to include the West End House, built by George Hildreth *c*. 1852, next door. Old-timers recall Dr. Furey's offices in this "Annex."

WINDSOR HOTEL, *c*. 1920. The home on the left was built in 1868 by iron and bronze foundry operator R.D. Wood on Windsor Street, which at first was called Wood. It was demolished in the 1930s. The Windsor Hotel remained popular through the 1960s, but, instead of celebrating its centennial in 1979, it was destroyed by a suspicious fire.

SEA CREST INN, *c.* 1923. The year before Cape May lost its beloved Windsor, this smaller hotel down Beach Drive at Broadway was torn down. In 1954, Aida O. Smith claimed that her establishment had been under continuous family ownership for 40 years. "Every Room an Ocean View" was the Sea Crest motto. (FB.)

COLTON COURT, *c.* 1933. This west end hotel on Beach and Patterson was created by joining the pre-1900 cottages of Thomas F. Kelly and Dr. A. New. The Thomas family owned Colton Court from 1945 to about 1970. In 1971, the hotel was torn down and replaced by a motel.

CONCORD INN, *c.* 1937. Back at Grant and North, this building resembles its Victorian neighbor the Alcott House, but does not appear on a 1932 aerial photograph. In November of 1942, owner M.B. Wagner sold the Concord Inn to a Presbyterian charity whose Cape May Point "Seaside Home" had been washed into the Delaware Bay by a March storm.

ELBERON, *c.* 1908. This boarding house opened on the new Congress Place in 1884. It was demolished to make room for a motel during Cape May's Urban Renewal about 1969. Thomas Hand, *Star and Wave* publisher, rescued the Elberon's right-hand neighbor by moving it to 33 Perry. Built for Eldridge Johnson *c.* 1880, the traditional seashore cottage now wears untraditional pink paint.

WYOMING, c. 1906. In 1879, Mrs. J.A. Myers established this small hotel in the middle of the block between Congress Street and Perry, on South Lafayette Street. It could accommodate 50 guests and was patronized by Baltimorians. In 1925, Wm. D. Vanzant advertised his 17th season as proprietor. Today the site is the Devon parking lot.

HOTEL DEVON, c. 1907–15. This Victorian hotel next to the Wyoming was owned and managed by Mrs. Garretson and Miss Hildreth in 1900. Today, the old Devon has been rehabilitated and is managed by a condominium association. Dubiously take note of the old sign: "Open All the Year."

20

THE RUDOLPH/ SEVILLA, *c.* 1906. In 1879, local architect Enos Williams built this hotel at 8 Perry to replace George Doughty's Avenue House, which had already been ablaze when Camden's steam engine rolled off the train on November 8, 1878. That night, all that remained of the neighborhood was a "flat surface of glowing embers," but no lives were lost. (EDH.)

RICHARDSON'S, *c.* 1914. This hotel at the end of Jackson Street across from Swain's may be the same structure that appears on an 1877 map as Cape May House. Richardson's served the African-American community as a hotel and saloon for over 40 years. Today, it holds shops. Underwood & Underwood of New York and London published this real photo postcard. (RE.)

21

BALTIMORE INN, *c.* 1906. Author George Thomas disputes local legend that this huge frame building was a "leftover" shipped from the Chicago World's Fair. We do know it opened on Jackson Street in 1893 and, thereafter, Southern families moved in for the season. In 1910, baby Tommy Penrose's mamma glued his photograph onto this postcard. In 1971, Baltimore Inn was demolished.

CARROLL VILLA, *c.* 1919. In 1882, veteran hotel-owner George Hildreth replaced his burnt cottage at 19 Jackson with this new-style small inn, a contrast to the huge pre-fire hotels. Targeting Baltimorians, he named his cupola-topped villa for Charles Carroll, Maryland's signer of the Declaration of Independence. In the 1890s, a new wing, heated bedrooms, and a larger porch were added.

VIRGINIA HOTEL, c. 1920s. Alexander McConnell was the first on Jackson Street to rebuild after the fire, hiring Enos Williams to design this flat-roofed bracketed villa called Ebbitt House in 1879. It was raised and improved c. 1895. In 1986, Curtis Bashaw's Chamberlain Hospitality Group invested $3 million to convert the aging Virginia into a neo-Victorian luxury hotel and restaurant.

GLENWOOD, 1913. This real photo card shows a noteworthy shingle-style hotel built and owned by important local contractor Enos R. Williams in 1890. In 1925, manager H.M. Macomber offered "Clean rooms, Home-cooking—Plenty of food. Rates $3.50 and $4.50/day." A parking lot now occupies this site on Hughes Street, near Decatur.

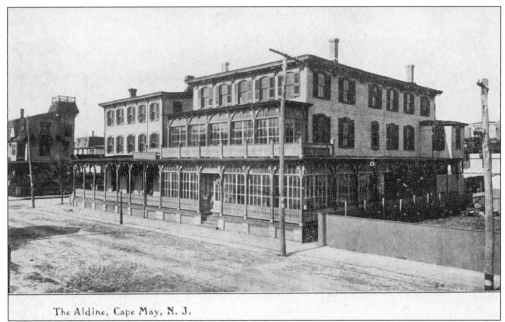

The Aldine, Cape May, N. J.

THE ALDINE/ ELWARD, *c.* 1906. Here at the intersection of Decatur and Columbia, the square-towered house has been replaced by the Presbyterian church parking area and the corner building, with a vacant lot. In 1900, Aldine proprietor Theo Mueller advertised, "First class cuisine, large airy rooms, terms moderate, steam heat, sunparlor." In the 1950s, low rents attracted summer waitresses from Kokes' and Youngbergs'.

The Lafayette. Cape May, N. J.

LAFAYETTE HOTEL, *c.* 1924. Where Decatur meets Beach Drive, on the old Columbia property, Victor Denizot built this L-shaped hotel in 1884. To see Stephen D. Button's original design in all its glory, look for earlier postcards. Here, the Lafayette has been "decolumned" by new owners Davis and Taylor in 1922. In 1970, it was replaced by the Marquis de Lafayette Motor Hotel.

OCEAN VIEW HOTEL, *c.* 1940. Pharmacist William Weightman's home was split in two and moved from Washington and Franklin to Beach and Ocean *c.* 1882. In 1963, when the Lafayette Hotel next door planned a motel addition, Rev. Carl McIntire saved the cottages by moving them to Trenton and New Jersey Avenues. Recently, the Girtons restored and reunited them as the Angel of the Sea.

Aug. 14, 1907. Star Villa, Cape May, N. J.

F. V. T.

STAR VILLA, *c.* 1907. This hotel right around the corner was also moved to the east end by Dr. McIntire and has now been renovated as condominiums. Our postcard shows the 1893 fourth-floor addition, but a few early Ocean Street cards picture the original 1883 design. Notice all the star embellishments added by Philadelphia architects Collins & Autenrieth.

25

The Colonial.   CAPE MAY, N. J.

COLONIAL HOTEL, *c.* 1910. In 1895, builders W.H. and C.S. Church opened this small Ocean Street hotel with its matching Queen Anne towers. Shown here is the south wing added in 1905 and, next door, the Stockton Baths rebuilt after the Great Fire. The 1942 Visitor Guide describes it as "cool and homelike," mentioning elevator service and rates "$23+up American plan/week."

THE BREXTON HOTEL
CAPE MAY, N. J.
Rates $2.50 and $3 per day
M. I. SENSOR.

BREXTON HOTEL, *c.* 1906. Cape May recycles! To make room for the railroad in 1890, the pre-1850 Delaware House on Lafayette Street was moved to Ocean and Hughes to become part of the Brexton, which was then torn down in 1907. Its parts became the (Colored) DeGriff Hotel on Corgie, the Terminal Taxi building on Washington, and the house still at 918 Stockton Avenue. (CMCHS.)

THE COLUMBIA, *c.* 1920s. Today, Victorian Towers occupies this Ocean Street site just across the Great Fire's boundary. The hotel opened as the Arctic in 1874. When the Chalfonte's Colonel Sawyer leased it in 1890, he changed the name to the Columbia. As the Sylvania, the aging hotel went from Lifeguards' Balls to the wrecking ball. Mecray's grocery was E-Z Market at the end. (FB.)

Stockton Villa.   Cape May, N. J.

STOCKTON VILLA/MACOMBER, *c.* 1920s. Mrs. Sara S. Davis opened this huge shingle-style hotel on the site of the former Stockton Hotel at the corner of Beach Drive and Howard Street just in time to accommodate the friends and families of servicemen crowding Cape May in 1918. The top floor shown here was destroyed by fire in 1938 and rebuilt.

HOTEL DALE, c. 1913. Our tour of Cape May's historic accommodations ends on Lafayette Street, east of Jefferson, where the White Hall was built in 1850 for Dr. Samuel S. Marcy, whose brick house still stands on the corner. In 1911, black entrepreneur E.W. Dale gave the old building new life as "the most finely equipped and most sanitary Afro-American hotel known."

HOTEL DALE. Perhaps this postcard came from the rack shown here on the check-in desk. Hotel Dale's long list of distinguished guests includes Dr. Booker T. Washington and Dr. W.E.B. DuBois. Their testimonials join those of physicians, a college president, and a bishop in Dale's lavish brochure. In 1936, the city razed Hotel Dale and today a motel replaces its tennis courts.

Two

Beach Drive and Promenade

Beach Avenue and Boardwalk.   CAPE MAY, N. J.

BEACH AVENUE, c. 1914. An 1879 West Jersey Railroad brochure describes a 50-foot wide graveled drive extending the length of the whole Cape May seafront and a 10-foot wide boardwalk sweeping along for nearly 2 miles. Our tour begins with the c. 1910 English country house-style Francis Hill home and, across Queen Street, the c. 1912 colonial revival Wm. Morice cottage.

BEACH AVENUE, c. 1923. This postcard of "colored nannies" pushing perambulators along the 900 block captures the essence of this quiet residential neighborhood. Local photographer W.F. Reupsch sent this view to the Albertype Co. in Brooklyn, a firm that fortunately did not subscribe to the common practice of erasing people and cars to keep the postcard from being "dated."

BEACH AVENUE, c. 1909. On the 1877 map, four houses show in this block stretching from Jefferson to Howard. The Joseph Lewis house in the foreground was built c. 1870. The "witch hat tower" identifies the first Macomber Hotel, whose motto was "Once a Guest, Always a Friend." Next door, the c. 1872 Henry Tatham house designed by Stephen D. Button later became the Macomber Annex. Notice the Stockton beyond.

STOCKTON AVENUE, *c.* 1907. These cottages were built on marshy land filled by developer Bullitt in 1872. The vacant lot held the Marine Villa until it burned in 1903. On this postcard, Alice reports, "Old Mr. Biddle was struck & killed by the 3-30 train yesterday afternoon . . . right back of our house," adding that his son Will wishes he had not run to see who it was.

BEACH AVENUE, *c.* 1913. Beyond the trolley rounding the bend at Ocean Street, this view looks east to the long band pavilion on the beach. In 1991, after Cape May completed the first stage of federally funded beach replenishment, the late "Doc" Jarden led an ambitious dune restoration effort. By 1998, over 174,000 sprigs of grass had been planted by more than 70 volunteer "Duners."

31

THE STOCKTON BATHHOUSES, *c.* 1909. The bathhouses destroyed in the Great Fire (see p. 15) were replaced in 1879 by these fancier red-roofed buildings designed by the Wilson Brothers, Philadelphia architects: 1,000 rooms plus a photograph gallery. When President Grant visited the brand-new Stockton Hotel in 1869, the first lady set tongues wagging by ordering red-and-blue flannel bathing costumes.

BEACH AVENUE, *c.* 1911. The photographer carefully avoided a gaping hole in the landscape, to the right, created when the Stockton Hotel was razed in 1910. Salvaged materials helped build several cottages that season. That same year, Cape May enhanced the boardwalk with ornamental arches and Beach Avenue with this welcome arch, all lit with rows of small electric bulbs.

BOARDWALK, *c.* 1911. While Joseph K. Hand's photographer was moving to his left, the young cowboy found a bench and lost a girlfriend. The building beyond the fence is the band pavilion at the foot of Guerney Street. Notice the trolley tracks along the beach side of the boardwalk and, in the distance, the Iron Pier and the columns of the Lafayette Hotel. (M & SW.)

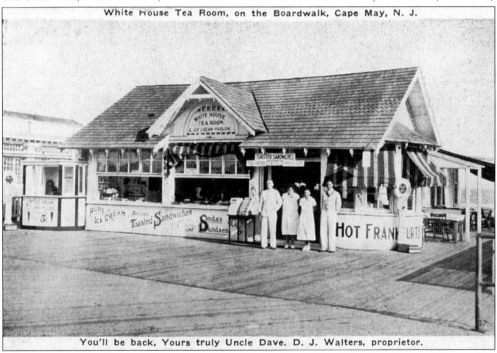

White House Tea Room, on the Boardwalk, Cape May, N. J.

You'll be back, Yours truly Uncle Dave. D. J. Walters, proprietor.

WHITE HOUSE TEA ROOM, *c.* 1925. Fast forward and here's Uncle Dave and his staff in front of the former band pavilion. His advertisement promised, "SATISFACTION! That's what you get when you eat Dunham's Hot Dogs served with Kokes' Rolls, Heinz's Mustard, Pickles and Chili Sauce." The name changed to Hartley's and the menu to seafood, steaks, and chops by 1954. (WHC.)

STOCKTON BATHS, *c.* 1911. Horse-drawn vehicles and horseless carriages had to co-exist on the dirt streets of pre-World War I Cape May. Perhaps the owner of that fancy "tin lizzie" has stepped into the Smith studios, at the left, where the sign reads, "PING PONG & POSTAL CARDS—TAKEN BY THE PAINLESS METHOD." Behind the baths is the Colonial with the Star Villa opposite.

STOCKTON BATHS, *c.* 1907. By 1878, over two thousand bathhouses lined the seafront. Ordinances regulated bathing: $5 fine for "skinny-dipping" between 5 a.m. and 7 p.m. (1865); $5 fine for persons over 20 on the street in bathing costume (1903). "Baths" rented cubicles, towels, and swimsuits to daytrippers and reserved space for cottagers who expected to find their bathing costumes freshly laundered daily.

BEACH BETWEEN OCEAN AND DECATUR STREETS, c. 1912. Beyond the lady about to have sea-soaked high-button shoes, hotels and cottages line Beach Avenue on what was the Columbia Hotel's front lawn before the Great Fire: Star Villa on Ocean Street, Weightman House halves, and Lafayette Hotel. Today, modern architecture fills this block, but, across Decatur, Denizot's 1879 Ocean View House remains.

LAFAYETTE HOTEL, AUGUST 14, 1911. Gov. Woodrow Wilson is addressing the crowd from the third balcony, after resting and dining at the hotel. His visit to Cape May County was requested by the Holly Beach Yacht Club, which was lobbying for Inland Waterway funds. After visiting Cape May's new harbor, the Governor left Schellenger's Landing on the fast yacht *Gibson Girl* for his tour. (EDH.)

The Boardwalk, Cape May, N. J.

BOARDWALK IN FRONT OF LAFAYETTE HOTEL, *c.* 1906. These demurely clad ladies out for a promenade would certainly be shocked to see the revealing summer fashions of today's boardwalk strollers. Collectors note: The publisher used an old view that included message space on this postcard's front and added the new correspondence/address back, which became legal in 1907.

P4101 Beach Avenue from Decatuer Street. Cape May. N. J.

BEACH AVENUE, WEST FROM DECATUR, *c.* 1914. Underwood & Underwood's real photo postcard is so clear that some of the signs are legible. On the pole, we learn, "CAPE MAY POINT CARS STOP WEST END OF PLATFORM." Arnold's advertises "SALADS— SEAFOODS OF ALL KINDS." Next door is "A. BARSA ORIENTAL STORE," and then "SHIELDS EXCELSIOR BATHS." King Cottage is next, at Jackson, with Uncle Dick's Baths beyond. (RE.)

36

BOARDWALK, *c.* 1914. Behind the young man vainly trying to impress the girls, we see Arnold's with new beer keg planters. Denizot called the building Ocean View Hotel when he built it on Great Fire ruins. By 1925, Henri's Palm Garden was offering music, dancing, and dining there and, in 1961, Henri's pianist Bobby Harris was playing Cole Porter when the authors first met. (RE.)

City of Tents in front of Stockton Surf Baths.

BEACH SCENE, LOOKING TOWARD DECATUR, *c.* 1911. On the back of this postcard printed by the Star and Wave Pub. Co. and mailed to Delaware on September 20, 1911, the message reads, "there is not one fourth this many people here now and only three or four tents on the beach." Time to promote the "shoulder seasons!"

BOARDWALK, ACROSS FROM ARNOLD'S, *c.* 1900. This postcard's undivided back with "This side for address" guarantees it was printed before March, 1907. The absence of automobiles suggests an earlier date for the photograph. City council had already added streetlights to Beach Drive by 1882. At the Iron Pier, Chong, Hop, Hing & Co., and neighboring shops offered fans and other exotic souvenirs.

IRON PIER FIRE, 1907. Chief Hanes reported for May 27, "Alarm turned in 1:58 p.m. Box 69 Iron Pier. Pier destroyed. Cause of fire—pot of tar boiling over on stove in the house. All apparatus in service." Smith Studios quickly printed this real photo card, which was purchased by a spectator who circled his own image and mailed the card to Comstock, New York on May 28.

Trolley Station on Boardwalk,
Cape May, N. J.

FRONT OF IRON PIER, *c.* 1913. When former tenant Schwartz moved back into the grand rebuilt pier, his Busy Corner claimed to be headquarters of souvenir postcards. Here, about five years later, Ping Pong Studio vies for that title and also offers "AMATEUR WORK DEVELOPED & PRINTED, ENLARGING, CABINETS, PING PONGS." Ping Pongs? Pier visitors could choose between two moving picture theatres. (FB.)

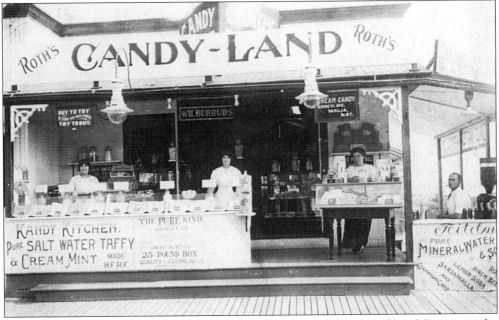

IRON PIER SHOP, *c.* 1913. Postcard Images' Patti and John Vierra in Gray, Maine were the lucky finders of this real photo postcard envied by local collectors. Roth's CANDY-LAND and Petroff's, its competitor, are gone, but several old-fashioned shops remain to sell Cape May visitors "fresh-made" fudge and salt water taffy. Today, the name Teitelman is linked with a school, instead of a soda shop.

BEACH AND JACKSON, *c.* 1908. This impressive cottage belonged to Wm. King, who owned the Excelsior Hot Baths next door in 1881. After the Arnolds sold Denizot's former Ocean View to the Borbachs, they turned this home into their Cape Club & New Ocean Terrace, featuring entertainment by the Baldwin Twins in 1941. Bathers welcome. Today, the lot holds a miniature golf course and a bar.

JACKSON STREET FROM THE BEACH, *c.* 1905. The towers next to the King Cottage belong to the Baltimore Inn across from the Seven Sisters of Atlantic Terrace. On the western corner is another curio shop: A. Barsa Direct Importers of Japanese Art. Barsa was also a local postcard publisher.

40

ATLANTIC TERRACE, *c.* 1910. The Great Fire destroyed E.C. Knight's 4-story, 250-guest Atlantic Hotel on this site. In 1891, Stephen D. Button designed these "Seven Sisters" for Knight, arranging them facing communal open space, so that their parlors and porches have an ocean view. Now mostly B&Bs, they are no longer identical septuplets.

BEACH AVENUE AND PERRY, *c.* 1913. Ping Pong Studios photographed this bevy of beauties in fashionable beach attire, all set to splash and float and fanny-dip in the Atlantic waves across the street. Uncle Dick's Bathhouses rented "SUITS and ROOMS 25¢—SPECIAL RATES FOR THE WEEK—MONTH—SEASON." Next door, another Japanese Store displayed trinkets and a full rack of postcards. (RG.)

41

BEACH AVENUE AND PERRY. In this post-1907 view, E.J. Scull is selling cigars, ice cream, and candies on the same corner occupied by Uncle Dick's Baths in the previous picture. Which came first? The closer mansard roof belongs to the Rudolph (see p. 21), and the next, to the 1879 Fryer's Cottage, near the 1878 fire's origin. That's Congress Hall on the left.

BEACH AVENUE AND GRANT, *c.* 1913. Our boardwalk promenade has taken us past Congress Hall and Windsor Hotel. Here, the trolley has crossed to the boardwalk's street side, heading to South Cape May and Cape May Point. Enjoyed as a social center for Greater Cape May's African-American residents and summer workers, the pavilion and beach shown were customarily "Colored" until *c.* 1960. (WHC.)

Three

The Endless Round
of Amusements

"THREE BELLES OF COOL CAPE MAY," c. 1900. As early as 1766, a *Pennsylvania Gazette* ad refers to Cape Island "where a Number resort for Health, and bathing in the Water." "Cool Cape May," coined in 1896, appears in red on this series of (six known) pioneer cards. Our earliest postmark is 1902, on a similar "Private Mailing Card—Authorized by Act of Congress of May 19, 1898."

Reclining Chairs and Shade Tents on Beach, Cape May, N. J.

STOCKTON BEACH, *c.* 1906. Beyond tent city, the Iron Pier stretches into the sea. On this site, Victor Denizot's 850-foot new amusement pier burned in 1878, but was quickly rebuilt. Cape May Ocean Pier Company razed Denizot's pier in 1884, replacing it with one 1,000 feet long and 30 feet wide. In 1909, a barge loaded with harbor jetty stones demolished the pier's ocean end.

The Life Boat, Cape May, N. J.

8/25/'05

We didn't find the "Widow." Hard luck. D.C.?

STOCKTON BEACH, *c.* 1905. On this Iron Pier, vaudeville replaced opera in the pavilion theatre in 1901, and by 1913 the pier entrance sign (p. 39) had changed to "MOVING PICTURES." Fully dressed ladies and clinker-built lifeboats are rarities on summer beaches today. Unlike our modern Beach Patrol, Victorian lifeguards spent the "bathing hour" on guard in boats just beyond the surf.

On the strand at Cape May, N. J.

STOCKTON BEACH, *c.* 1907. Not just for bathing, the beach is a place to "see and be seen," even if it means promenading in wasp-waisted gowns (and tightly laced corsets) during a heat wave. At sunset, Cape May sands become "flirtation walk." The buildings shown here beyond the parasol are on Stockton Avenue.

The Bathing Beach — Cape May, N. J.
A. Barso, Publisher.

This is where I play.
Gordon & Malny

CONGRESS BEACH, *c.* 1899. Beyond these charming children playing at the water's edge, this postcard's background provides a rare glimpse of now vanished buildings. Starting at the right, notice the Windsor, Wood house, Summer Station, and Railroad Excursion House. That tiny silhouette is the wooden elephant called The Light of Asia, which was built as a developer's attraction *c.* 1884 and razed in 1900.

Children, at the Beach, Cape May, N. J.

SANDCASTLE BUILDERS, *c*. 1906. The Rotograph Company in New York City shipped A.W. Hand's beach view to Germany where state-of-the-art printing presses created this postcard for the local publisher. In 1907, when *The Ocean Wave*, est. 1854, merged with *The Star of the Cape*, A.W. Hand joined the newspaper. The Hands ran *The Star and Wave* for four generations.

Bathing at CAPE MAY, N. J.

BATHING, *c*. 1910. Local papers did not seem to take note of this spacious, topsail schooner anchored off the bathing grounds. The four-legged sea dogs in the photograph are safe from fines or capture; Animal Control Officer Queenan wasn't even a gleam in his daddy's eye when this picture was taken.

FIRST AID STATION, *c.* 1920s. Who tended to splinters and scraped knees in this little red-roofed house with the roll-up canvas sides? Red Cross nurses! The Cape May branch of the American Red Cross hired the first one in 1909. In 1932, Mrs. Edith Carroll was on duty at this Red Cross Emergency Tent. Notice the billboards beside the new Stockton Villa. (EDH.)

REALLY COOL CAPE MAY, *c.* 1905. At least four different postcards of this king of the (ice) mountain "photo-op" were printed. The handwritten message on the front of a real photo card postmarked 1905 says, "A winter scene along the beach. The ice came down the Delaware." On the side of the Iron Pier, two Philadelphia clothing merchants advertise: Yates & Co. and Snellenburg.

Anniversary Day—May 10

COLUMBIA PARK, 1918. The pitcher winds up while the batter hopes to slam one over the fence in this real photo card looking from Columbia down Madison to Beach. Cape Island formed its first baseball club in 1866, led by J.F. Cake and Dr. James Mecray. The sport flourished here. Fans rooted for the Cape May Collegians at Columbia Park and, from c. 1932, Sea View Park.

Golf Club House, Cape May, N. J.

CAPE MAY GOLF CLUB, c. 1910. The club formed in 1897 with developer John C. Bullitt as president and Dr. Emlen Physick, vice president. Cape May Golf Club constructed a nine-hole course on Lafayette Street and hired Philadelphia architects to convert the c. 1870 Wales home into a clubhouse, which soon became the Cottage Colony's social center. In 1941, green fees were $1.50/day.

Congress Hall and Tennis Court, Cape May, N. J.

Atlantic Studios, Cape May, N. J.

CONGRESS HALL TENNIS COURTS, *c.* 1930. Tennis has been popular in Cape May ever since William Moore was tennis pro/manager of the Cape May Golf Club's clay courts. In 1961, Mr. and Mrs. T. Harris, Dr. and Mrs. Newcomer, and Robert Alexander donated part of the Physick Estate for a new tennis center, later dedicated to William J. Moore on his 100th birthday.

BEACH AVENUE AND BOARDWALK, CAPE MAY, N. J.

BABY PARADE, *c.* 1930. Cape May was promoting itself as Family Resort, rather than Victorian Landmark City, when Convention Hall ballroom's director of dancing started the "Juvenile Jubilee and Baby Parade" in 1928. This annual caravan of mermaids, cartoon characters, and clowns has been wondrous to behold ever since, especially *c.* 1935 when the author and sister were Mickey and Minnie Mouse.

CONVENTION HALL, c. 1918. This patriotic crowd in front of Convention Hall seems to be waiting for the Fourth of July parade. In 1917, the City had purchased the former Stockton Hotel's 434-foot-wide riparian rights for $20,000 from the estate of the late Dr. Emlen Physick and hired local contractor Sherman Sharp to build this entertainment pier in time for the summer season.

CONVENTION HALL, c. 1924. Various businesses rented shops in Convention Hall: Sawtelle's (pharmacy), Albed's (oriental rugs, linens, women's clothing), Ricker's (postcards, vacation needs, SKEEBALL). In 1925, Hunt's City Pier Theatre offered: Rin-Tin-Tin in *Tracked in the Snow*—the finest dog picture ever produced, Tom Mix in *The Lucky Horseshoe*, and the Our Gang comedy *Mary, Queen of the Tots*.

Interior of Convention Hall, Cape May, N. J.

CONVENTION HALL INTERIOR, c. 1919. Every summer Sunday, free concerts were held here with "Symphony Orchestra and Metropolitan Opera Artists." On every other evening, the municipal Dance Orchestra played for adult dancing, a custom inaugurated with the first City Ball on July 4, 1917. The hall decorations shown here might be for a dance or for the popular flower show.

INTERIOR, CONVENTION HALL, CAPE MAY, N. J.

CONVENTION HALL INTERIOR, c. 1928. Strict "floor managers" enforced the "adults only" rule on most evenings, but on Wednesdays and Saturdays one hour was set aside so that children could dance with the complete orchestra. On those afternoons, free dancing classes taught "skirt dance, nursery rhymes, kicks, twists, arm movements, Waltz, and Fox Trot." Friday evenings' Children's Review showcased budding talent. (FB.)

Band Pavillion, Cape May, N. J.

BAND PAVILION, *c.* 1916. Before Convention Hall, concerts were held at this pavilion (see p. 33),
which was one of several built on the beach front in 1891. Because the City did not own the riparian rights, this construction created controversy among some property owners. When the pier shown collapsed under a crowd watching a staged lifeguard rescue in 1925, 60 victims sued the city.

Interior Music Pavilion.
CAPE MAY, N. J.

BAND PAVILION INTERIOR, *c.* 1911. Music has enhanced this seaside resort's vacation experience ever since the Victorian hotels imported famous orchestras to entertain in their grand dining halls and ballrooms. Cape May's custom of providing free outdoor summer concerts, begun in 1891, continues today at the Rotary Bandstand. (RG.)

52

PORTER'S MARINE BAND, 1909. City council rejected the Clayton Band's low bid of $3,875 in favor of Porter's $5,000, justifying the extra expense to the taxpayers: "It is our duty to get the best we can for the money." The band shown in this real photo card by L.A. Skank of 607 Broad Street included 14 Clayton musicians. Admission for their July 24 Baseball Benefit was 10¢. (EDH.)

MARINE CASINO, c. 1913. Underwood & Underwood's real photo postcard shows the new amusement center built on the old Marine Villa lot at Howard and Beach, described in a message as "one of the chief attractions at Cape May—movies on the left—dancing on the right—and soft drinks in the little house under the windmill." Cottagers later enjoyed it as the Green Mill.

THE CASINO.   CAPE MAY, N. J.

THE CASINO, *c.* 1915. In 1912, Nelson Z. Graves tried to rejuvenate the New Cape May project by having this casino, designed by Lloyd Titus, built on landfill at Madison and Beach. In 1925, the Casino claimed to be "the only theatre south of Atlantic City where you may enjoy a play, not a motion picture, with professional players."

THESPIANS? Those look like stage sets in the background of this Ping Pong Studio real photo postcard. Could this be director Walter Greenough's Harlequins enjoying a picnic? By 1932, the Casino was called the Cape May Playhouse and, in 1954, was described as "the only legitimate theatre which once housed a carousel." Stars included Jessica Tandy, Gloria Swanson, and Burgess Meredith.

54

THE FUN FACTORY, c. 1913. The harbor dredge's tugboat docks beside this amusement casino opened on 2.2 acres at Sewell's Point by Nelson Z. Graves in 1912. When the ambitious New Cape May plan led Graves to a bankruptcy sale in 1915, the catalog listed "Fun Chase, comprising Roulette Wheel, Revolving Barrel, Razzle Dazzle, Large Sliding Boards, Soup Bowl, etc."

BUILDING THE FUN FACTORY, 1912. Ping Pong Studio sold this real photo postcard showing the double pergolas under which trolley passengers entered the amusement pier. The tower under construction had an upper viewing platform 85 feet above the water and was ablaze with electric lights at night. The South Pavilion held a large hall for concerts, minstrel shows, dancing, and roller-skating, with dining upstairs.

Schellinger's Landing. Cape May, N J.

SCHELLINGER'S LANDING, *c.* 1907. One of Cape Island's pioneer families developed this landing as a port and shipyard in pre-Revolutionary War days and it has continued as a boating center ever since. This view of Cape Island Creek looks north to Boathouse Row where the marina stands today. The Cape May Yacht Club docks are in the foreground.

SCHELLINGER'S LANDING.   CAPE MAY, N. J.

SCHELLINGER'S LANDING, *c.* 1918. This view from the bridge includes Yacht Avenue where the Coast Guard Auxiliary now owns one of the middle houses. York's Gas Station & Dock, at right center, rented boats from *c.* 1918 and by 1941, included "*MARLIN & CLOVER, SAIL YACHTS*"—For Charter by Day and for Moonlight Rides." The first dock has a diving board at this popular "swimmin' hole."

56

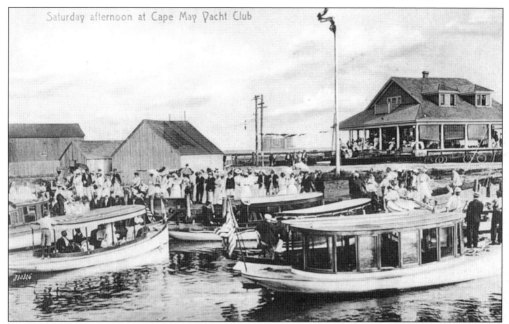

CAPE MAY YACHT CLUB, *c.* 1906. Dr. Emlen Physick donated the lot at the end of Washington Street for this clubhouse, which opened with a large membership of cottagers and residents in July, 1904. That year, Wilson Marshall's 188-foot, 3-masted schooner *Atlantic* won the Cape May Challenge Cup in a 300-plus mile race. The Cape May Yacht Club folded in 1925.

POLLY PAGE II ON HER AFTERNOON OCEAN SAIL, CAPE MAY, N. J.

THE *POLLY PAGE II, c.* 1930. Right at the foot of the Schellinger's Landing Bridge, vacationers boarded the *Polly Page II*, owned and operated by Capt. George Bohm. This gaff-rigged sloop offered two trips daily, to the delight of both passengers and sea-viewers. White-bordered cards like this date from 1915 to 1930.

Angling from City Fishing Pier, Cape May, N. J.

FISHING PIER, *c.* 1924. This pier behind Convention Hall was damaged by storms, including the 1933 "tidal bore," and rebuilt, until finally succumbing to the 1944 hurricane. Fishermen, hoping to land kingfish, weakfish, flounder, blues, or drum, paid a small admission and found bait and tackle available. The Episcopal minister started a "shark scare" each time he landed one on the beach.

TRIUMPHANT ANGLERS, *c.* 1920. Drum is the catch of the day proudly displayed on the boardwalk railing across from Arnold's at Decatur and Beach. Some of the proud fishermen in this real photo postcard include Sam Cliver—fish peddler (left), the Arnold brothers (middle), and Harvey Lewis (with corncob pipe). The largest black drum recorded from 1929 to 1939 in Swain's Fishing Contest weighed 93 lbs. (WHC.)

THE *BLACK GOLD*, c. 1926. At least 24 different boats issued cards like this one. Here, George Williams shows off both his daughter Dorothy and his new steamer *Black Gold*, which was reputed to have been a local "rum runner" during Prohibition. In the Depression, little son Harvey counted Reading Railroad "Fishermen's Special" passengers so that Dad would not waste precious money on extra ice.

THE *JACKIE B. II*, 1930s. Captain Buhalo's calling card starts, "My Business has been established since 1900. I have been pleasing and displeasing people ever since. I have lost money and made money. I have been cussed and discussed, knocked about, talked about, lied about, held up, flattered, robbed." It ends, "Forget your troubles and take my advice—FISH ON THE *JACKIE B. II*."

THE *RALPH J.*, *c.* 1930s. Ralph Johnson's postcards promise, "We will be looking for you on the Fishermen's Excursion, leaving Market Street Ferry 6.00 A.M. on Sunday, other days at 7.00 A.M." One satisfied customer scrawled this message: "This is the boat we where [*sic*] on our trip 40 miles out the ocen [*sic*] it is a lot larger than look as we had 200 abord [*sic*]."

CAPTAIN JOHNSON, *c.* 1938. Ralph's father Thomas built the *Ralph J.*, the *Vaud J.*, and this boat, which at 110 feet, claimed to be the "largest Party Fishing Boat on the N.J. Coast" in 1928. In 1938, Capt. Ralph W. Johnson's "Fast Twin Screw Diesel Power Yacht" offers "Good accommodations for ladies and children. Lines, Bait, Baskets and Refreshments. Boat fare $2."

Four
Streetscapes

WASHINGTON STREET, *c.* 1912. This street is one of the early ones named on Ezekiel Stevens's 1836 Cape Island survey. Shown here is the home across from the present post office and (never shown) George Allen House. It was built *c.* 1867 by Humphrey Hughes VII, who had been running the 125-room Tremont House next door at Frankin Street since *c.* 1850.

COLONIAL COTTAGE, *c.* 1910. To build the new high school (now Cape May City Hall) in 1918, this unusual home was moved to Della V. Johnson's property at 815 Jefferson, where it can still be seen behind the Washington Inn. In 1872, the owner was Mrs. LaGambie and next door was a REAL Colonial House, built by Memucan Hughes *c.* 1760s.

Washington Str., Cape May, N. J.

WASHINGTON STREET, FROM PERRY, *c.* 1908. Joseph K. Hand may have chosen this view for his patriotic postcard because it includes his father's jewelry store, shown on the left beside two other jewelry manufacturers. Next comes T. Mont Smith's *c.* 1881 confectionery and the Star and Wave building. On the right is W.J. Fenderson—Real Estate, a printing office, and, at Jackson Street, the Capitol Hotel.

BIRD'S-EYE VIEW, LOOKING EAST, *c.* 1907. That is the Capitol Hotel again at left center. By 1954, it housed Harry's (Reeves) Market plus a beauty shop and later, Barry's Clothes. The photographer may be looking down from the Congress Garage tower at this panorama, which includes the Star and Wave sign in the foreground and the many-columned Stockton Hotel in the middle distance.

WASHINGTON STREET, *c.* 1918. Could that be Thornton Pocher on his Indian motorcycle in front of John Dilk's Bicycles, Motorcycles & Repairs and Key Fitting at #304? Many of the shops shown on this Philadelphia-printed card are the same as those pictured in the earlier view on the opposite page, but Cresse Garage has moved into the vacant lot.

WASHINGTON STREET. CAPE MAY, N. J.

WASHINGTON STREET, *c.* 1914. In 1895, New Jersey Trust and Safe Deposit Company built this sturdy brick bank, adding iron grills to assure customers their treasures were secure. Gingerbread-trim on the house next door is appropriate, for it may be the oldest New Jersey bakery in continuous operation, starting as Essen's before the Great Fire and becoming Kokes' prior to World War I.

Hughes Street. CAPE MAY, N. J.

HUGHES STREET, *c.* 1911. This street started as a cowpath on tavernkeeper Memucan Hughes's plantation during the Revolutionary War era. When son Israel died in 1832, his widow divided this farmland into lots, setting aside a prime parcel near Ocean Street for her son Memucan II, a prosperous Delaware Bay & River pilot. Our postcard looks past the Cherry House toward Franklin Street. (M & SW.)

COLUMBIA AVENUE, FROM FRANKLIN, *c.* 1914. Having recently purchased and improved the old Columbia House on Ocean Street, early developers Bullitt & Fairthorne created this street in 1866. During the 1870s, another developer, Peter McCollum, built and sold two of the cottages shown here: #731–33, the corner 10-room twin-gable double house, and #725, a center-gabled Gothic cottage.

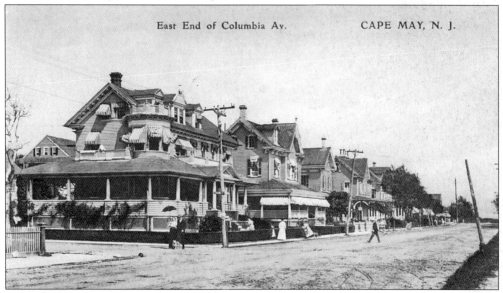

East End of Columbia Av.   CAPE MAY, N. J.

COLUMBIA AVENUE, *c.* 1910. If the photographer had swung his camera to his left, the 1872 Jackson's (gambling) Clubhouse would be in view. So far, no postcard of this Victorian landmark has surfaced. This postcard shows #701, Mrs. Harry L. Cassard's Teahouse in 1918, on the corner of Stockton Place. Next door, #705 is another McCollum development house, *c.* 1872.

COLUMBIA AVENUE FROM GUERNEY, c. 1909. These three first cottages were designed in 1867 for Philadelphia gentlemen and built by Hand & Ware, popular local contractors. The house in the foreground, #615, was later stripped of its ornate gingerbread porch decoration. The third house's porches had an unusual feature for Cape May: cast-iron columns and spandrels. Today, this row is B&Bs.

GUERNEY STREET, c. 1918. Look at all the "Things That Aren't There Any More" that show up in this postcard published by W.F. Reupsch, local photographer—the dirt street and row of trees, the second-story porch on the 1869 John B. McCreary villa in the foreground, the shingle-style renovations of #30 Guerney next door, the vacant Stockton Hotel lot, and the new Convention Hall.

Hand-colored

COLUMBIA AND GUERNEY, *c.* 1909. From the ornate cast-iron cresting atop its 60-foot tower to the graceful Gothic revival doors, this 1869 landmark shouts the Victorian motto: "Too Much Is Not Enough!" Architect Button and Philadelphia contractor R.J. Dobbins created this impressive villa for coal baron John B. McCreary. His son's house, built in 1873, is behind the trees next door.

Cottages on Guernay Street, Cape May, N. J

GUERNEY STREET, *c.* 1906. These eight gingerbread cottages were designed by Button in 1871 for developers Warne & Sewell, who built them with the same 25-foot setback as the neighboring McCreary villa. The massive hotel across the street gave them the name Stockton Row and, as shown on p. 15, both the Stockton and the Row barely escaped the Great Fire.

67

HOWARD STREET, *c.* 1909. The house in the foreground was reputedly built *c.* 1880 for Ann Buchanan, niece of James Buchanan, who was president of the United States just before the Civil War. That is the 1876 Chalfonte on the Sewell Avenue corner and those horse-drawn carriages on the left may be the ones that welcomed hotel visitors at Grant Street's Summer Station.

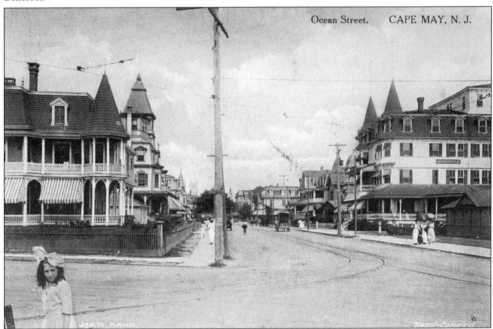

OCEAN STREET, *c.* 1913. By standing on the boardwalk, Joseph K. Hand's photographer captured this busy streetscape with the Weightman Cottage, the Star Villa, and, in the distance, the Church of Our Lady Star of the Sea tower on the left. Opposite, the dormered mansard roof beyond the Colonial belongs to Dr. Virgil M.D. Marcy's former pharmacy with its rare pre-fire storefront. (WHC.)

OCEAN STREET, *c.* 1922. Ice cream sales helped William Essen finance this Queen Anne-style cottage he built on the former Columbia Hotel grounds after the 1878 fire. An 1880 calling card from his Ice Cream Saloon on Washington Street promises, "Hotels & Cottages Promptly Supplied." The colonial revival home across the street is remembered as the office of Dr. Frank Hughes.

OCEAN STREET, *c.* 1906. This gull's-eye view from a Colonial Hotel tower shows Essen's home as the third in a row of mansard-roofed cottages. Across Columbia Avenue is the former home of Douglas Gregory, one of Cape May's many prosperous Delaware Bay & River pilots, and, next door, the Brexton. Congress Garage's tower juts above the horizon, with Quidort's 1896 auditorium to the right.

69

MERION INN, c. 1906. Cape May vacationers and residents have been "Meeting at the Merion" for conviviality ever since Patrick Collins opened this Decatur Street cafe in 1885. The chief steward of the posh Merion Cricket Club purchased the establishment in 1906, changing the name and adding a Philadelphia Main Line clientele. Signs read "PIEL BROS.- LAGER BEER" and "LADIES ENTRANCE."

DECATUR STREET, c. 1910. The popular and prolific Cape May photographer Walter Smith resided next to the Merion Inn. This postcard view is just down the street where the First Presbyterian Church sits at the Hughes Street corner. Opposite, #120 belonged to Mrs. M. Knerr, whose 518 Washington Street shop advertised in 1901: "Millinery—DRY GOODS—Ladies' & Gent's Furnishing Goods."

JACKSON STREET, *c.* 1912. This is the seaside resort's oldest street, part of Cape Island Road, which was surveyed in 1783. Our view looks toward its end where Ellis Hughes's Atlantic Hall, the FIRST beachfront accommodations, offered seabathers in 1801 "Fish, Oysters, Crabs, and good Liquors." Whiskey dealer Christopher Gallagher had #45, on the left, built in 1882. Beyond is the Virginia.

Jackson Str.   CAPE MAY, N. J.

JACKSON STREET, *c.* 1910. Mecray Pharmacy's postcard shows many of the same houses from the opposite direction. Behind the cast-iron fence is one of the Seven Sisters, built near the former site of Atlantic Hall. Beside the Queen Anne-style cottage with its witch-hat tower, at #24, Tom and Sue Carroll inaugurated Cape May's burgeoning bed and breakfast industry in 1971.

PERRY STREET, c. 1908. According to historian Robert Alexander, this was probably the "new road" which ran from the Cape Island Creek Bridge to the Atlantic Ocean and opened with the first Congress Hall in 1816. This Stockton Row-type cottage at #11 has been "modernized" beyond recognition. The tiles visible next door are reputedly from the Centennial Exhibition held in Philadelphia in 1876.

PERRY STREET, c. 1910. Shown here from North Street are old summer boarding houses, including Parris Cottage and Clinton Hotel at South Lafayette Street. That 85-foot tower on Congress Hall Garage was the top of the 1875 Sea Grove pavilion, purchased for $400 by George Twitchell at the 1882 auction and moved from Cape May Point. It became a landmark to ships at sea.

PERRY STREET, *c.* 1906. Today, this house near West Perry Street is one of the Victorian seaside resort's picturesque "Painted Ladies." It was built for Isaac Pepper in the late 1860s, a period of notable growth for Cape May. In 1868, 40 new cottages were built in the city and 25 more, just beyond. The bridge crosses the creek that helped delineate Cape Island.

EXCELSIOR BUILDING, WEST PERRY, *c.* 1907. C.S. Newell's nephew wrote on this advertising postcard: "This is our Skating Rink—the second floor. The first floor is my Uncle's livery stables and Black Smith Shop. Those are his new horses. Certainly is a dandy place." Historian Karl Dickinson adds, "This is where we always watered our horse on our way home from market."

CONGRESS PLACE, *c.* 1918. When sugar tycoon E.C. Knight decided to rebuild fire-ravaged Congress Hall closer to the beach, room was left to create Congress Place and build this row of houses *c.* 1881. Visible here are the E.C. Knight and Joseph Evans Italianate villas, the eclectic Dr. Henry Hunt cottage, the Elberon Hotel, the Pavilion tower (behind), and, at Perry Street, Mecray's Pharmacy.

CONGRESS STREET, *c.* 1910. This postcard looks beyond Nelson Z. Graves's sundial to the hedges of the Edwin C. Knight home shown above. On the opposite corner is the American bracketed villa with its ornate two-story porches and striped cupola roof, built for Jacob Neafie *c.* 1865 (see p. 12). A horse and buggy heads down Congress Street towards the Windsor Hotel. (EDH.)

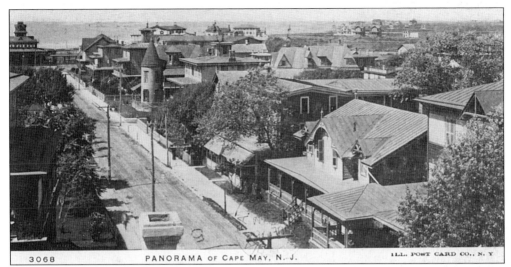

PANORAMA, *c.* 1899. Can you guess the cameraman's vantage point? He looks down South Lafayette at cottages belonging to Devon Hotel (foreground), Wyoming, unidentified, N.Z. Graves, (across Congress Street) Joseph Leedom, Ferguson (on Windsor), Dailey (obscuring the authors' home), and, across from Grant Street Summer Station, Lancaster. Above Leedom's tower is the Railroad Excursion House and, in the far distance, the elephant.

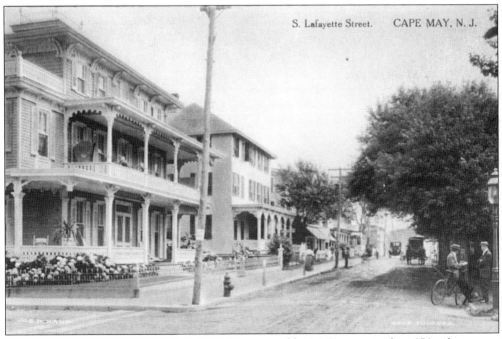

SOUTH LAFAYETTE STREET, *c.* 1910. First owned by M. Stanton in the 1870s, this corner cottage was purchased in 1897 by Philadelphian Nelson Z. Graves, a paint manufacturer and real estate speculator. It joined many of its neighbors on the Freeman Auction block during Graves's 1915 bankruptcy sale. Mr. Barnett moved the house next door to #231–33 Windsor, beside the Sewell mansion, *c.* 1918.

Mansard

Windsor and North Sts.

Cape May

S. C. Henry Proprietor

MANSARD, c. 1910. This boardinghouse is not really on the corner, but when Samuel Henry had the *Star and Wave* print his postcards, he also owned the Blue Pig next door, which is said to have been moved from Congress Hall lawn where it was Henry Cleveland's notorious gambling club c. 1850s. The wealth that built the Mansard in 1877 came from the Slaymaker's lock company.

The NORTH WINDSor -- Corner of North and Windsor Ave. -- is a quaint old Cape May mansion built about 1867 by a sugar cane king. It was originally part of Congress Plantation and was moved to its present site in 1878. Its spacious verandas with their elaborate hand carved railing are typical of the Cape May architecture of that period. One block and a half to the beach, close to shopping, churches and boardwalk activities.

NORTHWINDS, c. 1960. This narrow building surrounded by wide porches, across from the Blue Pig, reminds us that Victorians considered their verandahs outdoor living rooms, whiling away summer hours there as they rocked, read, visited, and carefully avoided the sun. This lot was owned by H. Gresse in 1872. A house appears on the 1877 map, supporting the McDevitt's story above.

NORTH STREET, #219, 1908. Real photo postcards like this are often one of a kind. By 1903, an inexpensive camera designed to take postcard size negatives and specially sized developing paper encouraged amateur photographers. North Street's quiet residential neighborhood is filled with surprises—this roof with decorative shingles and so many finials, federal houses next door, and a globe hitching post, opposite. (M&SW.)

WINDSOR AVENUE, #217–19, c. 1907. The house on Ping Pong Studio's real photo card was built c. 1876, when the street was named Wood. Guests could hear horses whinnying at Congress Hall stables in the block beyond. In 1881, it was "Seabrook," with M.A. Camp, proprietress. The wooden awning is still intact today; but General Sewell's mansion and Cape Island Creek bridge, at left, have vanished. (RE.)

Broadway Street Scene, Cape May.

BROADWAY, *c.* 1906. Visitors refer to Cape May's many-hued cottages as Painted Ladies. Local gossip claims this house, #201, was home to another kind of painted ladies—"Ladies of the Night." The bridge shown crosses Cape Island Creek, euphemistically nicknamed "Stinky Crick." After complaints about its use as an "open sewer," the creek was piped and filled from Broadway to Perry in 1927.

BEACH AVE. & BROADWAY, CAPE MAY, N. J.

BROADWAY, *c.* 1912. Our streetscape tour ends with Villa Nova, built overlooking neighboring South Cape May *c.* 1890–1905. Gambrel roofs were fashionable then. In 1918, George Rutherford was proprietor. By 1932, the name was Ocean Villa and the cupola was gone. The motto of Mrs. S. Malloy, the final owner, was "Rich in the Things that Make People Happy." The villa was razed in the 1960s. (RG.)

Five

Places of Worship, Learning, and Government

POST

PARISH OF
The Church of the Advent
CAPE MAY, N. J.
REV. PAUL STURTEVANT HOWE, PH.D.
RECTOR

Church Open All the Year

Services

Holy Communion · · · · 7.30 P.M.
　(8.00 A.M. from November to June)
Second Service and Sermon, 10.30 A.M.
Sunday School · · · · · · 3.15 P.M.
Evensong · · · · · · · · 4.00 P.M.

Ye Olde Church of the Advent
Cape May N J

PRESBYTERIAN/EPISCOPAL CHURCH, c. 1930. This building was constructed on Lafayette Street in 1853 after the local congregation was finally able to break away from the mother church at Cold Spring. Builder Peter Hand crowned the church with an exotic revival cupola. The Presbyterians moved out in 1899 and, thanks to benefactress Annie Knight, the Episcopalians worshiped here c. 1903 to 1953. (Both sides of the card are shown.)

PRESBYTERIAN CHURCH, *c.* 1908. The Cape Island Presbyterian Church, renamed the First Presbyterian Church of Cape May, purchased the Hughes and Decatur corner lot in 1892 for $6,500 and hired ecclesiastical architect Isaac Purcell to design this stone church. Its congregation and pastor have offered hospitality as "The Visitors' Church" since the first services in 1899. They bought the manse next door in 1904.

World War Monument, Gurney St., Cape May, N. J.

CAPE ISLAND BAPTIST CHURCH, *c.* 1920. Baptists were also on the move, leaving their 1879 wooden Gothic church at #727 Franklin for this stucco-covered Spanish Revival-style Sunday school built on the vacant Stockton Hotel property next to the shingle-style house in 1916. They added the church in 1937. Mecray Post #40 GAR and the Progressive League dedicated the monument in 1923.

80

ST. MARY'S ROMAN CATHOLIC CHURCH, *c.* 1910. Cape Island's first Catholic church was built on Washington Street's south side in 1848. In 1870, the renamed Church of Our Lady Star of the Sea was moved across to its present site and enlarged. See its twin at Cape May Point—St. Agnes's, the mission church. Rev. Dennis S. Kelly, shown, became pastor in 1900.

CHURCH OF OUR LADY STAR OF THE SEA, *c.* 1918. The *c.* 1870 rectory stayed, but in 1911, when construction of a grand new church began, little St. Mary's was moved toward Lafayette Street to become a chapel and hall. Philadelphia architect George Lovatt designed this granite and limestone Romanesque landmark to accommodate five hundred worshipers in the church and three hundred more in the chapel below.

METHODIST EPISCOPAL CHURCH, *c.* 1906. Methodism started on Cape Island in 1810, when Revolutionary War patriot Memucan Hughes invited circuit preachers to his home. In 1843, Methodists built a church on Franklin Street, but in 1854 they bought the Washington Street *c.* 1844 Presbyterian Visitors' Church. The parsonage, razed *c.* 1918, and Colonial Cottage (see p. 62) are adjacent.

FIRST M.E. CHURCH AND HIGH SCHOOL, *c.* 1923. The Methodists had the ubiquitous Stephen D. Button renovate the church *c.* 1867 and church member Enos Williams remodel it again in 1893, adding the triple-arch entrance. Atlantic City architect S. Harry Vaughn designed the high school, which was built on the former site of Colonial Cottage *c.* 1918. In 1961, it became Cape May City Hall.

HIGH SCHOOL, *c.* 1914. Since *c.* 1970, an Acme supermarket has occupied the site of Cape May's first high school, shown here. W.H. Church & Bro., builders of the Colonial Hotel, constructed the school for $35,000 in 1901, following the design of Philadelphia architect Seymour Davis. It became an elementary school when the new Cape May High School was built.

COLUMBIA AVENUE, #715, 1914. This Button-designed cottage built for John Tack *c.* 1872 by local contractor Joseph Q. Williams is greatly admired today for its remarkable rose garden. Young ladies once were taught piano and Latin here. "S.H.C.J.," plus M.M. Mary's message about a "retreat" and "Monsignor McDevitt" on this real photo card, suggest the house was church-owned.

83

The Alcott Vacation House.   CAPE MAY, N. J

JOS. K. HAND.

HUGHES STREET, #615, *c.* 1911. Louisa May Alcott had been dead for over 20 years before this postcard, but the popular writer probably inspired the name of this boarding house for "little women." From *c.* 1890 to 1909, the pre-fire cottage was owned by the Episcopal Diocese of Pennsylvania, serving as the GFS Holiday House and winter chapel. By 1932, it was Dormers Hotel.

LIVING ROOM, G.F.S. HOLIDAY HOUSE, CAPE MAY, N. J.

GFS HOLIDAY HOUSE INTERIOR, *c.* 1940. The old Baltimore Hotel (see p. 16) on the opposite side of Hughes Street at #644 became the new home for the Girls' Friendly Society in 1910. By the time these bobbysoxers were photographed, over 14,000 girls, mothers, and children had vacationed there. They still do, but they no longer march seaward in matching yellow bathing caps.

CITY HALL, *c.* 1908. When the city constructed Franklin Street School (right) in 1867, Cape Island had 217 pupils. The very first school had been built privately in 1835 a few lots away. On Washington Street, the city hall/fire department/police station/municipal court went up in 1899. In 1924, when the fire department "motorized," the beloved white firehorses retired. The building came down in 1970.

POST OFFICE, *c.* 1907. Most of the stamps found on our postcard collection were purchased here at #210 Ocean Street. This building has also housed the telephone company, U.S.O., and restaurants. The post office moved to the new Focer-Mecray building on Washington Street in 1923 and to the current building *c.* 1938. Ellis Hughes became Cape Island's first postmaster in 1804.

COAST GUARD, CAPE MAY, N. J.

COAST GUARD, *c.* 1920. The U.S. Life Saving Service constructed this building at #1111 Beach Avenue for $7,000 in 1890. Historian Ralph Shanks calls this Cold Spring station a Bibb #2 type. Of 22 lifesaving stations of this design by architect Albert B. Bibb, nine were in New Jersey. This one became the first Kiwanis-owned clubhouse in the United States in 1937.

The Breeches Buoy in Action.   AT CAPE MAY N. J.

BREECHES BUOY, *c.* 1906. Though these generic cards are found with various shore resort names overprinted, rescue drills like the one illustrated did take place on Cape May County beaches. A *c.* 1890 photograph shows crowds on the lawn of Cape May Point's Shoreham Hotel, now St. Mary's by-the-Sea, watching as the "victim" suspended in a breeches buoy is hauled to safety.

Six

All Aboard for
Cape May

ENJOYING A RIDE,   CAPE MAY, N. J.

BOARDWALK, *c.* 1907. During the Golden Age of postcards in Cool Cape May, getting there was half the fun. Yes, this pampered trio in the fancy wicker rolling chair is being pushed along on *our* boardwalk, not Atlantic City's. Another postcard, published by J.J. Spencer Jr., shows the same vehicle approaching Jefferson Street. The message suggests that Ross "come and make 50¢ a day."

IN FRONT OF STOCKTON BATHS, 1903. Kids used to yell, "Get a horse!" to passing autos. The pony in this real photo card views his tin-lizzie neighbor apprehensively. Jess Rutherford maintained a stable and took the adventurous "to ride horseback at the edge of the tumbling waters along a windswept beach, to thread an old logging road through holly woods to cranberry swamps," *c.* 1927.

SAME SPOT, WINTER, *c.* 1927. "Jingle bells, jingle bells . . . in a two-goat open sleigh." Perhaps her pout will change to a smile when this little miss cracks the whip and Billy Whiskers and Nanny, with bells on their horns jingling, pull her wicker sleigh down snowy Beach Avenue. Photographer Walter Smith kept a pet monkey in his studio rafters. Were these goats props?

June 1906

...get frightened...

INSIDE SMITH'S STUDIO, 1906. Speaking of props, notice the photographer's free ad on this one. With "automania" sweeping America during postcards' Golden Age, private studios like Smith's used the theme in real photo cards. Large publishers like Tuck created entire series poking fun at the new vehicles, with the Ford as a prime target. Henry Ford's 1905 race on Cape May beach is legendary.

LAFAYETTE HOTEL, c. 1907. Here in another photograph taken by Walter Smith's "Painless Method," three jaunty gentlemen pose in front of the Lafayette's shaded verandah. We bet one of them is the proud owner of the auto at left. If only color photography had been invented so that Smith could have shown the hotel's gold with brown and red trim paint in the background. (EDH.)

Pa. R. R. Station, Cape May, N. J. *DEAR MA THANK YOU FOR SENDING IT RECEIVED MY AUTO SOON J. THORNTON POCHER COME DOWN*

GRANT STREET STATION, *c.* 1905. When the railroad finally arrived in Cape Island in 1863, jubilant crowds greeted the steam train at the terminus of the track near Broadway and the beach. In 1867, West Jersey Railroad built its Sea Breeze excursion house there. Popo's card shows the view from his South Lafayette Street window: Grant Street Summer Station, built in 1876.

PENNA. R. R. EXCURSION STATION AND THE WOOD FAMILY RESIDENCE, CAPE MAY, N. J.

GRANT STREET STATION, *c.* 1911. Pennsylvania Railroad's architect, Joseph Wilson, designed both this station and Stockton Baths. When the little boy who wrote the postcard above was about 90, he relished the memory of a clam shell fitting his hand so perfectly as he aimed for the station windows! Across from Pochers', the 1870 mansion is industrialist Lea's, not Wood's.

READING RAILROAD STATION, *c.* 1928. On June 23, 1894, just hours after workers laid the last track, the first train chugged through an evergreen welcome arch at this new station on Washington Street amid great hoopla. Now Cape May had two competing railroads. The 1923 Focer-Mecray building, opposite, held the post office, meeting rooms, and "The First Ford Agency in America—Est. 1903." (WHC.)

READING TERMINAL, WASHINGTON STREET, CAPE MAY, N. J.

READING TERMINAL, *c.* 1906. Daniel Focer was offering Fords starting at $268.05 F.O.B. in 1925. Before long, the popularity of the automobile forced the two arch rival railroads to merge, creating the Pennsylvania-Reading Seashore Lines in 1933. That was the end of Grant Street Station. Visible past Reading Terminal are St. Mary's, Chas. Campbell's Real Estate & Ins., and the pavilion tower. (RE.).

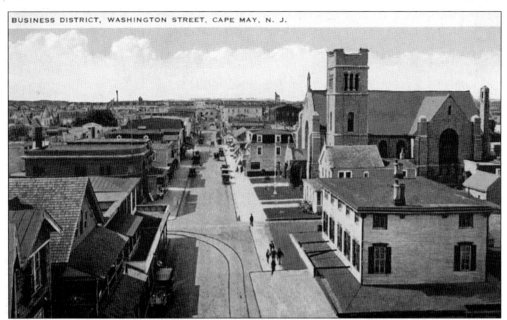

BUSINESS DISTRICT, *c.* 1925. Reading Terminal was razed in the late 1940s and replaced with the building now located across Lafayette Street at the new railroad terminus. Passenger service, finally run by Conrail, ceased on October 2, 1981, but will be resurrected by Tony Macrie's Cape May Seashore Lines. What's missing on this card? Delivery boys bicycling from the railroad's Western Union office.

COLONIAL HOTEL, *c.* 1915. That may look like MAC's Trolley, but it's really the Cape May, Delaware Bay, and Sewell's Point Railroad turning from Beach Avenue into Ocean Street. The previous card shows the next turn at Washington Street. In 1902, Reading Railroad sent four hundred gandy dancers to quickly lay Ocean Street track linking the terminal with the beachfront line to Cape May Point.

Beach Avenue, Cape May, N. J.

BEACH AVENUE, c. 1916. The trolley on the right may either turn into Ocean Street at the track junction just beyond the boardwalk arch or continue straight ahead to Sewell's Point. A second trolley has passed the band pavilion next to the *future* site of Convention Hall Pier. Perhaps those straw-hatted gents are strolling to the Iron Pier trolley station (see p. 39).

BEACH AVENUE, c. 1920. Both fires and storms shaped the nation's oldest seaside resort's destiny. This northeaster was a bit less voracious than the big storms of 1944 and 1962, but it still gnawed on trolley tracks and took chunks out of the boardwalk. Though Convention Hall and the New Stockton Villa appear unscathed, other real photo postcards show Beach Avenue yards flooded.

SEWELL'S POINT, *c.* 1905. Today the U.S. Coast Guard owns Poverty Beach where the Atlantic meets Cold Spring Inlet. The point is named for General Sewell: Civil War leader, U.S. Senator, West Jersey Railroad Superintendent, and important Cape May developer. In 1869, visitors coming by carriage on Beach Drive's new extension to Faucett's Fish House here chose *live* fish for the cook to prepare.

SEWELL'S POINT BOAT LANDING, *c.* 1910. With quick access to the ocean, this soon became a popular port for yachtsmen. Vacationers who wished to go for a sail found yachts like Faucett's *Harriet Thomas* shipshape and waiting. Sewell's Point was also the terminus for the trolley until the link with Schellinger's Landing in 1913 completed the belt line around the city.

BOAT LANDING, c. 1909. The trolley brought travelers right to the dock where, for 50¢ round trip, they could board a steam launch for Holly Beach. Since the sign reads "For Cape May," this postcard from Wildwood publisher R.W. Ryan probably shows Wildwood Crest dock, rather than Sewell's Point Landing. The other sign might advertise the Fishing Banks. (FB.)

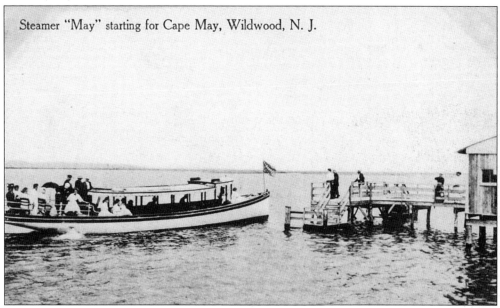

THE STEAMER MAY, c. 1912. Little steamers like this one were links in a transportation chain that extended up the Jersey coast. By railroad and launch, a hardy summer vagabond could travel from Cape May Point all the way to Atlantic City. This card's stamp box gives the postage to distant places: "Domestic Canada Cuba Mexico, Hawaii Philippines Porto Rico 1 Cent. Foreign 2 Cents."

THE MAY, *c.* 1915. A large party of vacationers enjoys the sea breeze on the trip from Sewell's Point to Wildwood. The captain has added an upper deck and, perhaps inspired by the recent *Titanic* disaster, conspicuous life preservers. Historian Richard P. Matchner gives the departure times for the *May*: 9:10 A, 12 M, and 2:45 P.

THE STEAMBOAT CAPE MAY, *c.* 1908. For just $1, excursionists traveled in style from Philadelphia to Cape May Point on the 280-foot-long sidewheel steamer *Republic* built at Wilmington's Harlan & Hollingsworth shipyard in 1878. New Cape May developers renamed her *Cape May*, sold her to New Yorkers *c.* 1904, and the old *Republic* became the *Dreamland* at Coney Island pier.

Seven

The New Cape May

DREDGE WITH TUGS, 1905. The shape of our resort was changed just after 1900 when what a Pennsylvania Railroad promotional booklet describes as "a strong and progressive band of moneyed men" saw the potential of the wetlands and sounds between Madison Avenue and Sewell's Point. Their plan was to buy 5,400 acres, dredge a 35-foot-deep, 500-acre harbor, and create 7,500 lots with the fill.

The Boardwalk near Sewell's Point — Cape May, N.J.
A Barsa, Publisher

BOARDWALK, *c.* 1905. These strollers have just passed the lifesaving station (p. 86) and fresh landfill as they return from inspecting the New Cape May project's progress. In 1903, Cape May City Council extended Beach Avenue, boardwalk, and bulkhead and built the Madison Avenue sewage pumping station. A holiday was declared for the christening of the huge dredge *Pittsburgh* by America's Cup hero Capt. Charlie Barr.

Dear Mary 85 8/10 per. Come down for the summer on me. Harry

HOTEL CAPE MAY, MARCH 1906. Harry's real photo card shows how far the building has progressed since Cape May Real Estate Company's president, Peter Shields, broke ground in September 1905 for this centerpiece of the New Cape May. Construction was plagued with problems, including strikes. In May 1906, a portion of the building collapsed; in September, the dredge *Pittsburgh* sank.

BOARDWALK, *c.* 1914. Compare this postcard with the one opposite. The boardwalk arch frames massive red brick Hotel Cape May, with Peter Shield's home in the foreground and George Boyd's elegant cottage beyond. The railroad bed is abandoned; new tracks cross Beach Avenue closer to Madison and continue up New Jersey Avenue to the Fun Factory. Ladies now wear hobble skirts.

RESIDENCE OF PETER SHIELDS, *c.* 1909. Cape May Real Estate Company's 1903 promotional brochure predicted erection of "palatial residences" in the New Cape May. In 1906, project architect Lloyd Titus designed this colonial revival as the first house on the prime beachfront lots. Shields was a Pittsburgh real estate entrepreneur backed by former-senator William Flinn and other Pennsylvania capitalists.

HOTEL CAPE MAY, *c.* 1913. The grand opening was finally held on Easter Sunday in 1908, over a year behind schedule. Cape May had hotels that were large and luxurious in its past; now it had one that was "distinctly a Metropolitan hotel, absolutely fireproof" and thoroughly modern. Construction and furnishing expenses reached over a million dollars, double the estimate.

HOTEL CAPE MAY PORCH, *c.* 1912. This 350-bedroom hotel with its elegant interior was the talk of the town. Its popularity was exploited by postcard publishers, who produced more cards featuring Hotel Cape May than any other local subject. Approximately a dozen views focus on the broad verandahs and terraced entrance designed by Pittsburgh architect Frederick Osterling.

HOTEL CAPE MAY LOBBY, *c.* 1908. Imagine yourself as a privileged guest standing beneath the glowing stained-glass dome. Huge matching fireplaces flank the entrance, just beyond this postcard view. Cross the classical terrazzo floor past (faux) Italian marble columns with gilded capitals and register at the reception desk beside the grand stair's ornate iron railings.

HOTEL CAPE MAY INTERIOR, 1909. Pity the poor concert-goer stuck behind a lady wearing a plumed chapeau. It looks as though the resort's entire population has crammed into the lobby for this event, including Popo (see p. 4), who is mugging for the camera from the second row. The photographer faced east, capturing architectural grandeur beyond the crowd and a bit of wicker under it.

HOTEL CAPE MAY DINING ROOM, 1908. Manager John P. Doyle, formerly of Washington D.C.'s New Willard Hotel, has seen to every detail. Easter lilies and azaleas decorate all tables. Each place is precisely set with new monogrammed silverware, sparkling crystal, and china bearing the mermaid-topped Hotel Cape May crest. The staff stands at attention awaiting Opening Day guests.

JAMES TYNDALL RESIDENCE, c. 1921. Meanwhile, back on the East Cape May landfill, building was slowly progressing. This view of #1120 New Jersey Avenue, with Hotel Cape May in the background, shows a c. 1913 colonial revival home far less pretentious than Peter Shields's. Dr. R. Walter Starr's cottage down the street at #1500 was the very first house on the tract in 1906. (WHC.)

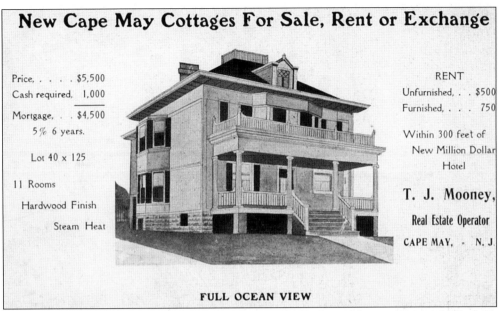

New Cape May Cottages For Sale, Rent or Exchange

Price, ... $5,500
Cash required, 1,000

Mortgage, . . $4,500

5% 6 years.

Lot 40 x 125

11 Rooms

Hardwood Finish

Steam Heat

RENT

Unfurnished, . . $500
Furnished, . . . 750

Within 300 feet of
New Million Dollar
Hotel

T. J. Mooney,

Real Estate Operator

CAPE MAY, - N. J.

FULL OCEAN VIEW

NEW CAPE MAY COTTAGE, *c.* 1906. This rare New Cape May card was published for Thomas J. Mooney, one of eight contractors listed in *Cape May, Queen of the Seaside Resorts* as builders of 21 identical New York Avenue houses started in 1909. Compare this artist's rendering with an actual development house at #1021 New York Avenue, noting neighborhood variations. (EDH.)

NEW YORK AVENUE AND HARBOR ENTRANCE, 1913. Joseph K. Hand captured two striking additions to the local landscape on this scarce postcard: the row of look-alike New Cape May houses and the new harbor's recently completed long jetties. Cape May Real Estate Company planned 7,500 lots on the landfill, locating the largest on Beach and Cape May Avenues. (WHC.)

BEACH AVENUE, c. 1912. The first New Cape May lot sold was this one at Beach and Baltimore, beyond Hotel Cape May. The buyer was George Boyd, general passenger agent for Pennsylvania Railroad—one of the project's major promoters. Boyd's perfectly symmetrical Georgian revival home was constructed in 1911. General Sewell's son built his shingle-style cottage next door in 1912.

BEACH AVENUE, c. 1911. The absence of Sewell's house dates this card, which views the same row of New Cape May cottages, looking west past #1601. At 50 by 150 feet, these oceanfront lots are the largest on the tract. The boxy structure before Boyd's home was the first of the cottages to be built and belonged to Dr. Davis, a pioneer plastic surgeon.

NEW JERSEY AVENUE, *c.* 1916. The mysterious four-story building behind the trolley is the help's quarters of the Cape May Hotel. No old-timer seems to recollect the structure. We suspect it was salvage from the 1910 Stockton Hotel demolition. The N.Z. Graves 1915 auction catalog describes a large dining room and laundry on the first floor and 80 bedrooms upstairs.

FARMSTEAD BY THE SEA, *c.* 1911. One of the suppliers for Hotel Cape May was N.Z. Graves's dairy and poultry farm on Seashore Road in Cold Spring, managed by J.P. Mackissic. A 1909 newspaper ad boasted that the "aggregation of healthful, cheerful and well groomed cattle" and the "collection of Leghorns and Wyandottes" (25,000 chickens) were the finest in the world.

DREDGE *NELSON Z. GRAVES*, *c*. 1912. In 1909, after president Peter Shields resigned, Cape May Real Estate Company's New Cape May stagnated. Gentleman farmer/paint manufacturer N.Z. Graves came to the rescue. First, he bought their electric plant. In 1911–12, he acquired Reading Railroad's trolley lines and Senator Flinn's holdings. As Graves's namesake deepened the harbor, development was revived. (RE.)

Club House of the Corinthian Yacht Club.   CAPE MAY, N. J.

CORINTHIAN YACHT CLUB, *c*. 1913. Yachtsmen had helped lobby U.S. Congress to enact legislation needed for creation of the new harbor and, as it neared completion, they formed a second yacht club. With N.Z. Graves's backing and Commodore R. Walter Starr's leadership, they built the Corinthian Yacht and Country Club at the end of Yale Avenue.

U. S. S. FANNING, AT OPENING OF GOVERNMENT'S $1,300,000 HARBOR OF REFUGE, CAPE MAY, JULY FOURTH, 1913. FIRST WARSHIP TO ENTER NEW JERSEY INLAND WATERWAYS.

WARSHIP IN CAPE MAY HARBOR, 1913. After investing more than $1 million in the construction of the harbor and jetties, the U.S. Government sent the *Fanning, Jenkins, Vixen,* and submarines to join in the opening day celebrations. Their crews marched in the spirited July 4 parade led by the Washington City Band and joined the athletic events, as jubilant crowds cheered.

THE HARBOR, *c.* 1920. The new Harbor of Refuge and the discovery of a 30-mile-long scallop bed off Cape May stimulated development of a fishing industry. By 1914, Cape May was the port for the New England mackerel fleet, which utilized a special Reading Railroad spur for shipping, and Joseph Wilson had built a wharf for his Cape May Fisheries.

ADMIRAL HOTEL, *c.* 1932. This jigsaw puzzle has a wooden back and is packaged in a thin box with a postcard back glued to the top, suggesting that it was to be mailed like an ordinary postcard. No doubt, this novelty was a souvenir from the hotel gift shop. 1932 Admiral ads promised "accommodations of the highest type" at "Rates Exceedingly Modest." (RG.)

ADMIRAL HOTEL, *c.* 1932. Our New Cape May chapter ends with this view of cottagers and hotel guests attentively waiting for divers to plunge into the famous "Outdoor Sea Water Swimming Pool." New Cape May never became the "Newport of New Jersey" and this landmark hotel was demolished in 1996, but we're left with elegant east end cottages, our Harbor of Refuge, and fond memories.

Eight
World War I and Cape May

BOARD WALK AND BEACH AVENUE, U. S. ARMY GENERAL HOSPITAL NO. 11.
CAPE MAY, N. J.

BEACH AVENUE, 1918. N.Z. Graves had lost his office and his farmstead, 475 lots, 24 cottages, the Casino, Fun Factory, and about 625 acres at the 1915 receiver's sale, but in 1917 he was still in control of Hotel Cape May. Graves offered the property, including help's quarters and garage, to the U.S. Surgeon General for hospital use, charging $99,000 annual rent.

Stairway, Main Floor, U. S. A General Hospital, No. 11, Cape May, N. J.

STAIRWAY, U.S. ARMY GENERAL HOSPITAL #11, 1918. Refer to page 101 to recall earlier times when fashionable belles made grand entrances and vacationers headed for summer amusements descending Hotel Cape May's impressive marble stairway. The hospital's first 34 patients arrived on April 1, 1918, from Baltimore's Fort McHenry. A soldier and Red Cross nurse pose here beneath Christmas garlands.

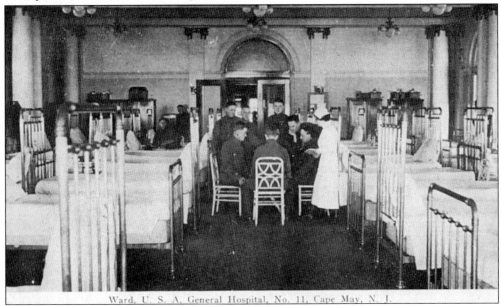

Ward, U. S. A. General Hospital, No. 11, Cape May, N. J.

WARD, U.S. ARMY GENERAL HOSPITAL #11, 1918. Rows of brass beds fill the ballroom and any music will have to come from those windup Victrolas atop the wardrobes in the background. That is Nurse Mary Barkham supervising while her patients enjoy a board game. "Isn't this a good looking ward. Of course you recognize yours truly," she writes on a folder version of this view.

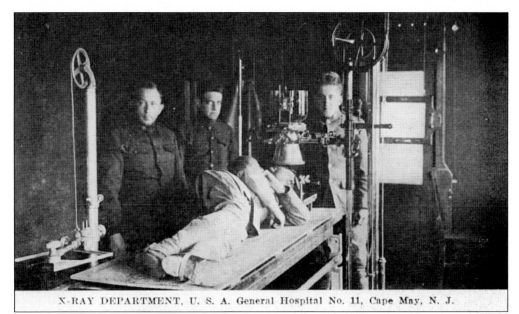

X-RAY DEPARTMENT, U. S. A. General Hospital No. 11, Cape May, N. J.

X-RAY, U.S. ARMY HOSPITAL #11, 1918. This contraption may look like something from Dr. Frankenstein's laboratory, but it must be the latest in Army technology. According to historian Larry Paul's research, the hospital military staff included "20 Medical, 8 Sanitary, 3 Dental, 2 Quartermaster Officers, 52 Nurses, 206 Medics, 1 Dietitian, 4 Motor Transport, and 48 Quartermaster Enlisted Men."

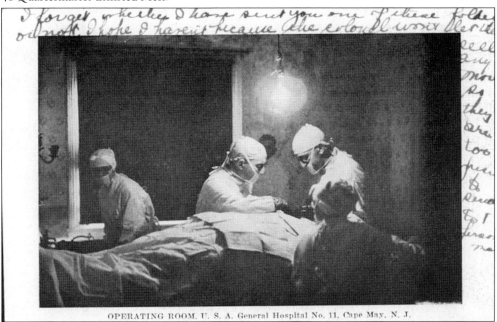

OPERATING ROOM. U. S. A. General Hospital No. 11, Cape May, N. J.

OPERATING ROOM, U.S. ARMY HOSPITAL #11, 1918. Many patients were doughboys who had survived the horrors of life in the trenches: machine guns, barbed wire, mustard gas, and seas of mud. At #11, R&R meant restoration and recuperation. Military staff was augmented by 27 civilian aides, plus 77 Hotel Cape May employees, including engineers, firemen, chambermaids, waitresses, a butcher, a baker, and a cook.

SECTION BASE, U.S. NAVY, 1918. Sailors have hauled their cots, duffel bags, and gear outside for "airing day." The building is the Fun Factory (see p. 55) which was abandoned and sand-filled in 1917 when the Navy arrived in search of a site for a base. The amusement park's conversion was imaginative: skating rink to mess hall/barracks, stage to galley, Barrel of Fun to brig.

SECTION BASE RUINS, 1918. On July 4, when nearly all the sailors were marching in a patriotic Cape May parade, the former amusement park caught fire. After racing back to Sewell's Point, some sailors tried to rescue clothing and provisions. Others tackled the dangerous job of saving fuel and explosives, but no lives were lost. Several real photo cards picture the destroyed base.

SECTION BASE, U.S. NAVY, 1918. This real photo card shows the new base being constructed after the July 4th fire. Corinthian Yacht Club, shown at center (see p. 106), was immediately established as Navy headquarters and tents were erected in its back yard as temporary housing for sailors not quartered at Wissahickon Barracks. C.Y.C. became a boys' camp c. 1925 and was razed c. 1940s.

PULLING TARGETS, SECTION BASE, c. 1918. The sailors built the Rifle Range themselves out of concrete mixed with salt water, constructing it for about a fifth of contractors' estimates. Men from the base, Wissahickon Barracks, and Philadelphia Navy Yard qualified as marksmen, sharpshooters, or experts here. There was fierce rivalry during the Division and Ship's Team Competitions.

NAVAL AIR STATION, *c.* 1919. The photograph for this Albertype Co. postcard was taken from high up in the Hotel Cape May. It looks down on the cottage at 1515 New Jersey Avenue surrounded by wet landfill. In the distance, the commandeered Corinthian Yacht Club is to the left of the new Section Base 9. The dirigible hanger, completed early in 1918, is on the right.

CAMP WISSAHICKON BOAT DRILL, *c.* 1918. In July 1917, four hundred carpenters with two hundred helpers began building a Naval training station on Henry Ford's farm, which was located near where the Garden State Parkway ends today. These Navy "boots" are learning seamanship on Cape Island Creek, west of the drawbridge. That's George T. Roseman's dock on the left and Nelson Graves's Farmstead in the distance.

CAMP WISSAHICKON KNOT-TYING CLASS, *c.* 1918. The potential market of three thousand seamen assigned to this U.S. Naval Training Station inspired publication of over 50 different postcard views, ranging from buildings to various drills. This is an Underwood & Underwood card, printed in color. Enlisted men built Section Base 9 for $46,627; contractors constructed Wissahickon for $1,500,000.

CAMP WISSAHICKON CLOTHING INSPECTION, *c.* 1918. This row of tidy sailors and their shipshape gear is shown on one of the plentiful Albertype Co. postcards. When Camp Wissahickon was dismantled in 1919, materials from structures like this barracks were used for new Cape May construction, including houses on Windsor Avenue. One building was moved to Cold Spring to become the "speakeasy" Sunny Hall.

CAPE MAY SUBMARINE BASE, N. J.

SUBMARINES AT BASE 9, *c.* 1918. These subs had their home port across Cape May Harbor from Wissahickon Barracks at Section Base 9 which directed sea activities and supplied personnel, equipment, and provisions to the "mosquito fleet" of about 30 minesweepers and patrol boats guarding the bay and seacoast. The USS *Savannah* served as mothership for six O-class American submarines.

U. S. COAST GUARD FLEET, BASE NINE, CAPE MAY, N. J.

U.S. COAST GUARD BASE, *c.* 1930. When the Coast Guard took over Naval Base 9 in 1925, eighteen 75-footers like these dressed ships shown above, several small fast boats, and the 157-foot cutter *Kickapoo* were stationed at Cape May harbor. During Prohibition, from 1920 to 1933, the Coast Guard went to war with the bootleggers, but the clever and speedy rumrunners frequently escaped capture.

NAVAL AIR STATION, *c.* 1918. There were 12 seaplanes, a dirigible, and a kite balloon at the air station when it opened in November 1918. The hangar measured 250 by 133 feet with a 66-foot clearance to accommodate the dirigible ZR-2. On its trial flight, however, ZR-2 crashed into the English Channel. Cape May's Lt. Charles Little was one of the 44 casualties.

NAVAL AIR STATION HANGAR, *c.* 1918. This real photo card captures docking of a non-rigid airship, probably a C-3 blimp. As the Navy developed airship use for anti-submarine warfare, this hangar proved too small for larger dirigibles. In 1930, Capt. Anton Heinan of the *Shenandoah* leased it to construct baby blimps. A fire hazard, the obsolete hangar was razed in 1941.

SEAPLANE, *c.* 1918. In 1925, the Coast Guard transformed the naval airfield and hangars into a seaplane station. After a Bermuda-bound airliner crashed off the New Jersey coast, the Coast Guard sent four large seaplanes to Cape May. From 1928 to 1934, the Chamber of Commerce leased 95 acres for a county airport. Atlantic Coast Airways converted five Army bombers into airliners there.

NAVAL HOSPITAL AMBULANCE, *c.* 1918. The back of this AZO real photo postcard says, "My father Richard F. Dawson is in the driver's seat." Dawson parked his ambulance beside Camp Wissahickon's hospital near a tall pole flying the Red Cross flag. The other Navy hospital, at Section Base 9, was converted from the old Sewell's Point waiting station for just $900 in 1917. (CMCHS.)

CAPE MAY GENERAL HOSPITAL No. 11
Weekly Auto Trip to Wildwood, N. J., February, 1919

GENERAL HOSPITAL #11, 1919. This postcard printed by the Jewish Welfare Board takes us back to the former Hotel Cape May where the patients are about to depart for the Soldiers' and Sailors' Club in Wildwood. As guests of honor, the boys will be treated to a chicken supper followed by an evening of music, games, and conversation. The hospital closed on July 20, 1919. (RE.)

Y.M.C.A. Headquarters

YMCA HQ, 1918 (see p. 30). "Claude old boy" received this real photo card showing one of many Cape May buildings used to accommodate the needs of servicemen crowding our resort by the thousands. Cottagers provided housing for officers and their families. City officials turned over Convention Hall to the War Camp Community Service. At Camp Wissahickon, the YMCA and K. of C. had centers. (RE.)

COMMUNITY HOSTESS HOUSE, *c.* 1918. Built at Columbia and Franklin Streets as marble merchant John Freely Jacoby's summer cottage, the Community Hostess House offered hospitality to homesick servicemen. Cape May's young ladies had the patriotic duty of keeping the boys happy and entertained. Their mothers tackled more serious wartime tasks, winding bandages, knitting mufflers, and promoting Liberty Loans.

CONCRETE SHIP, 1926. When the experimental S.S. *Atlantus* was launched in 1918, World War I was over. She brought two shiploads of servicemen home from France and helped rescue a sub crew before she was scuttled. In 1926, Col. Jessie Rosenfeld of Baltimore towed her to Cape May Point to be a dock for a proposed Cape May-Lewes ferry, but the 250-foot-long freighter ran aground.

Nine

On the Outskirts
of Cape May

11737 Rustic Gate Entrance to Sea Grove, now Cape May Point *May-6-1906.*
Philadelphia,
So romantic. E *Pa.*

SEA GROVE GATE, *c.* 1906. In 1875, Alexander Whilldin and his wife, Jane Stites, conveyed 266 acres of ancestral land to the Sea Grove Association to establish a planned religious community. The prominent Presbyterian founders included local pharmacist Dr. V.M.D. Marcy and Philadelphia merchant John Wanamaker. Sea Grove's architect J.C. Sidney designed this once impressive gate.

Boat Landing at Lily Lake, Cape May, N. J.

A. W. Hand, Cape May, N. J.

LILY LAKE, CAPE MAY POINT, *c.* 1906. This view captures the two area attractions most often found on postcards: the half-mile-long freshwater lake and (see p. 2) the historic lighthouse. Both Seagrove's boathouse and gate show architect Sidney's use of natural tree trunks and branches. The 1881 Seagrove auction catalog lists three sailboats and five rowboats with the "Rustic Boat House."

Villa Maria by the Sea, Cape May Point, N. J.

VILLA MARIA, *c.* 1930. The 1875 Sea Grove House, the Carleton from 1881 to 1910, had 126 bedrooms, a 250-seat dining hall, a 340-foot piazza, and amenities such as a music pavilion, 2 billiard rooms, and 4 bowling alleys. Temperance laws hastened its downfall. Sisters of the Immaculate Heart of Mary bought the hotel in 1914. Erosion forced its abandonment in 1937.

SEASIDE HOME, c. 1910. The list of old Cape May Point's charities is impressively long. This one began in 1879 when ladies from Philadelphia's Presbyterian Orphanage bought an ice house, moved it to a donated lot, and offered vacations to women and children of limited means. Supporters like the Wanamakers helped Seaside Home grow, but the sea claimed it in 1942 (see p. 19).

VILLA LANKENAU, c. 1906. In 1890, John D. Lankenau built this spacious beachfront retreat at Coral Avenue for the staff of his German Hospital in Philadelphia. Our postcard shows Lutheran deaconesses, brought from Germany to serve as nurses, who cherished their vacations here. This villa burned in 1908, but was rebuilt. As Chelsea Apartments, it was a victim of the 1962 storm.

Cape May Point from Lighthouse, Cape May, N. J.

PANORAMA FROM LIGHTHOUSE, *c.* 1922. At far right is the oceanfront cottage of Sea Grove's founder, Alexander Whilldin. Its neighbor, the Carleton, is just out of view. In 1890, Wanamaker and friends gave that large dormered house (left) to First Lady Harrison, creating a scandal. The long building along the trolley tracks once served as movie theatre, art studio, and lifeboat house.

St. Mary's by the Sea.   CAPE MAY POINT, N. J.

ST. MARY'S-BY-THE-SEA, *c.* 1911. In 1890, with America's First Family as neighbor/tourist attraction, the Shoreham Hotel was opened and Cape May Point promoted. John Philip Sousa honeymooned there. After a short span *c.* 1898 as the Home for the Aged and Infirm Colored People, the Shoreham was purchased for $9,000 by the Sisters of St. Joseph in 1909, becoming St. Mary's-by-the-Sea.

124

WILBRAHAM PARK, *c.* 1922. This tattered postcard pictures West Cape May's "pride and joy" shortly after its dedication, when the plane trees were mere saplings. Philadelphia industrialist J.W. Wilbraham, whose mansion overlooked the park, donated it to the community. West Cape May became a borough in 1884, but from 1898 to 1909, the post office was named for its leading family: Eldredge.

BEAN THRESHERS, *c.* 1930s. Since 1985, Wilbraham Park has hosted the popular Lima Bean Festival where crowds sample lima recipes and crown the Lima Bean Queen to music of the Lima Bean Polka. According to farmer Les Rea, Cape May County once had 3,000 acres in limas, producing 1,200 to 2,000 pounds of beans each. This card is one of more than 36 block prints by Katherine Schmucker.

COLD SPRING PRESBYTERIAN CHURCH, 1907. The "Old Brick Church" shown on this real photo postcard was constructed in 1823, but Cold Spring Presbyterian Church was organized in 1714, making it the nation's fifth oldest Presbyterian church. In 1718, a log structure became its first home. Tombstones in the nonsectarian cemetery bear venerable names of Cape May's founding families.

CABIN CITY, c. 1930s. Not far from "Old Brick" and the famous freshwater spring that gave the village its name, weary travelers still recovering from the Great Depression found this "Nice Place for Nice People" along what is now Route 9, then the main road between Cape May and New York City. Today, 18 modernized original cabins are available for Roadside America fans.

HEDGE GARDENS, FISHING CREEK, c. 1946. For over 50 years, no road trip would be complete without visiting the botanical wonders on Tabernacle Road. In 1928, Gus Yearicks began to fill his nursery with over 175 topiaries, including a stagecoach, bicyclist, sailing ship, and baseball game. This real photo souvenir postcard shows Gus with the *Queen Mary*, which took him 18 years to shape.

TABERNACLE M. E. CHURCH, Erma, N. J.

TABERNACLE CHURCH, ERMA, c. 1917. Methodism began in Cape May County in 1778 when Abram Woolson, the area's first convert, welcomed a preacher to his Fishing Creek home. The postcard shows the fourth Tabernacle Church to be erected on land donated in 1803 by Memucan Hughes, builder of Greater Cape May Historical Society's Colonial House. In 1966, a fifth church replaced this one.

WILDWOOD VILLAS, c. 1933. In the 1920s, Joseph Millman purchased Fishing Creek land and started a development of inexpensive summer bungalows, naming it as a suburb of the popular Wildwoods. The 1942 *Cape May County Resort Guide* promoted it as a "charming bayside resort. Ideal vacation spot, this complete, modern community has stores, churches, a post office and convenient transportation."

VILLAS POST OFFICE, c. 1932. By 1954, half its residents stayed year-round and Millman advertised, "YOUR DREAM HOME COMES TRUE—4 rooms and bath, large lot, near beach—All for only $2,995. Small down payment—easy terms—low taxes." Our tour of Cape May and vicinity finishes at Postmaster Harry R. Murray's General Store, just in case you need to mail a postcard.